REFLECTIONS
OF AN
OPTION SELLER

REFLECTIONS

OF AN

OPTION SELLER

THE RISE, FALL, AND RETURN
OF A COMMODITY MARKET MAVERICK

JAMES CORDIER

Forbes | Books

Published by Forbes Books, Charleston, South Carolina.
An imprint of Advantage Media Group.

Forbes Books is a registered trademark, and the Forbes Books colophon is a trademark of Forbes Media, LLC.

Printed in the United States of America.

10 9 8 7 6 5 4 3 2 1

ISBN: 979-8-88750-460-5 (Hardcover)
ISBN: 979-8-88750-461-2 (eBook)

Library of Congress Control Number: 2024911543

Cover and layout design by Matthew Morse.

This custom publication is intended to provide accurate information and the opinions of the author in regard to the subject matter covered. It is sold with the understanding that the publisher, Forbes Books, is not engaged in rendering legal, financial, or professional services of any kind. If legal advice or other expert assistance is required, the reader is advised to seek the services of a competent professional.

Since 1917, Forbes has remained steadfast in its mission to serve as the defining voice of entrepreneurial capitalism. Forbes Books, launched in 2016 through a partnership with Advantage Media, furthers that aim by helping business and thought leaders bring their stories, passion, and knowledge to the forefront in custom books. Opinions expressed by Forbes Books authors are their own. To be considered for publication, please visit **books.Forbes.com**.

AUTHOR'S NOTE

To keep this memoir authentic and accurate, I requested that
Forbes Books make no changes to my original manuscript.
These are the facts as I remember them, with only a few names
changed for privacy.

JAMES CORDIER

This book is dedicated to those who chart their own course in life and in business. Those who are compelled to stray from the herd to blaze a new path. Those who question the status quo in search of new opportunities, and propel society forward as a result.

To all the mavericks, where would the world be without you?

CONTENTS

CHAPTER 1

EYE OF THE STORM

Friday, November 16, 2018
3:30 p.m.

Standing in front of my office window on the 23rd floor of the SunTrust Building and looking out over Tampa Bay, I'm trying to figure out how to address a harsh reality. I haven't slept in two nights, and I'm struggling to think of something to say that will explain the situation we're in. The situation I'm responsible for.

For years, I've been recording brief videos once or twice a month for my clients. Always speaking off the cuff, I updated them on market developments, explained what I got right or wrong, and provided my outlook for the future. Those videos helped to assure the people who trusted me with their investment – and I knew each one of them by name – that I was the right person to manage the portfolio.

Justin, from our tech team, is setting up the camera on a tripod in front of my desk. We've done this a hundred times before, but today everyone in the office has a look of disbelief.

This time is different.

I managed $250 million in total equity for OptionSellers.com, a trading firm I founded and built over the last two decades. I have an experienced team in place, hundreds of loyal clients, and a waiting list full of people interested in becoming clients.

We're a small operation compared to most well-known trading firms, but I thought we were the perfect size. Large enough to have some clout on the trading floor, but small enough to trade nimbly in and out of positions without moving the market. We had performed very well for our clients up until this week, amassing a 10-year annualized return of 17 percent.

I have benefitted personally, as well. I'm one of the premier option traders in the country, appearing on Bloomberg, CNBC, and Fox Business. My market commentary appears in prestigious investment publications, such as The Wall Street Journal and Forbes. McGraw Hill is interested in publishing a fourth edition of my book, *The Complete Guide to Option Selling*. My wife Krista and I live in a beautiful bayfront home in nearby Apollo Beach. To celebrate our two-year anniversary, I recently purchased a 72-foot Princess yacht that I christened *The Krista Renee*.

At age 56, life couldn't have been any sweeter.

"Ready when you are," says Justin from behind the camera.

I have always shot straight with my clients. When I fell short of expectations, I acknowledged it. That is what I'm here to do today. But I still have no idea what I'm going to say this time. There are no words that will help.

I take a seat at my desk, sip from a glass of water, and take a deep breath as I try to mentally prepare for what I'm about to do. My gaze happens to land on the shelf displaying an intricate model ship that was handcrafted by my father. He knew very little about commodity investing, but his sage wisdom from an early life at sea translated well into my profession. I often used nautical metaphors for trading: Chart your course. Maintain a steady hand at the helm. Keep an eye on the horizon. Always be prepared for rough seas.

The aphorism on my mind this week has been *"any port in a storm."*

"Okay, Justin," I say. "I'm ready."

I'm not ready. It feels like I'm about to jump out of a plane for the first time.

"Good afternoon, this is James Cordier of OptionSellers.com with a market and account update for November 16, 2018. Needless to say, the events of this past week have been incredibly devastating for our clients, who I rarely call clients. Around the office, and sometimes on phone calls, I refer to our clients as family. And on what we call a 'new account client call,' I often thanked and told the new client that 'we were so happy that you were joining our family.'

"Dr. Steve, and your wonderful wife in L.A., I'm happy to share with you that Kriss's ailments that we discussed so eloquently are gone. She's feeling just great.

"Kurt and Grace in Michigan, so sorry to say that we never got to go bass fishing. I wound up walleye fishing on Lake Erie. It was not nearly as satisfying as had I got to go with you.

"Our client in Kansas City, thank you so much for the barbecue sauce. I will enjoy it and think of you always in the future. For Larry and Rex, it looks like I owe you a Cuban sandwich."

This is excruciating. There's no need to keep mentioning individual clients. But for some reason, I continue.

"For our client in Marseille, my wife and I were certainly looking forward to joining you on the French Riviera, it is so beautiful.

"Our clients on the Gold Coast in Australia, I was hoping to see that beautiful sunset you spoke of so many times. More locally, Troy, I was really hoping to become a boating enthusiast with you. That I will miss.

"John, we talked about you a lot in the office. Not sure you knew it, but your name was 'Boca.' And though you thought I didn't enjoy our afternoon chats, I actually did. Good luck in Texas.

"Also here locally, the biggest hockey fan in the world, Jeff, you know who you are, all I wanted to do was sit with you and watch a game. The next time I'm at the arena, I know you'll be there, and I'll pretend I was sitting next to you...."

Don't break down, man. Hold it together....

"...So many of you chose to entrust in us the ability to navigate in the world of investing. Practically every time we spoke of positioning your account the best we could, I referred back to my father who used to sail an 800-footer on the Great Lakes, and I always talked about steering your investment like a boat. I remember so many times saying if you're steering the wheel and someone's watching you and you're making small turns, that's good. And if you're making large turns, that's probably what you don't want to see.

"In the *Wall Street Journal* this week, it spoke on and on about the movements in the crude oil market and the natural gas market. It talked about the incredible volatility that cost funds and fund managers and hedge funds their livelihood, and clearly, they had a livelihood because they had investors.

"This rogue wave that I was unable to navigate has likely cost me my hedge fund, and the reason why I had a hedge fund is because of you, our clients. I promise you every day when I woke up and I would check the markets, I was checking for rogue waves. Often when I spoke to you on the phone, we'd be on speaker, and I had my two hands in front of me like they were on a wheel of a boat. And I always want to make the best turns for you, and I tried making small ones, and I truly invested your funds like you were family. I am so sorry that I was unable to manage the rogue wave that hit us this week…."

Why did I call it a hedge fund? It's not a hedge fund. I'm losing focus here. I'm rambling.

"…I wish I could name you all by person right now, all 290 clients of ours. You are my family and I'm sorry that this rogue wave capsized our boat.

"In the coming days and weeks, our office doors will be open, our phones will be answered, any questions that you might have. My staff — Rosemary and Alicia and Matt and Michael — will do their best to answer questions you might have and somehow help."

I can't believe the words are coming out of my mouth. I can't believe they're true. I've seen other high-profile traders in this position over the years, but I never thought it would be me.

"I want to thank you all for becoming part of our family. I wish you all the best… I am so sorry for not managing our ship and keeping her afloat."

CHAPTER 2

UN-NATURAL GAS

The price of natural gas had risen 50 percent in less than three days, and it was still unclear why. That kind of rapid gain is not unheard of in this market, and it was certainly within our range of plausible risk scenarios. That's why we had an exit strategy. However, in any of the flash-rally situations I was prepared for, we would have to know the catalyst for the event.

Natural gas is the third most actively traded physical commodity futures contract in the world. It is used globally by fossil fuel companies, utilities, and other industries to hedge risk, as well as by speculators chasing profit. Surely the price couldn't increase by half for no reason. There must be some tangible event driving up the market, but it still has not revealed itself.

When the price began to rise Friday, November 9th, it was a relatively modest rally. We checked all the usual suspects to find out what was causing it but found nothing out of the ordinary. There had been only minor changes to the temperature forecast, no hurricanes approaching, no major production outages, pipeline issues, etc. No unusual trading activity that we could see. There was no clear fundamental driver or technical indication of a larger move to come.

Our research and my experience told me this was just the ebb and flow of a listless market. Perhaps an energy fund made a large purchase in a SWAP or OTC transaction, causing a temporary bump in the futures price that would subside after a few days. That sort of thing happened all the time.

The following week, natural gas continued moving higher and higher, still without explanation.

I attempted to buy back our short positions through the usual channels, but there was nobody willing to sell. Market-makers and speculators were baffled by what was happening and, as a result, liquidity evaporated. Natural gas option markets, which typically had a fraction of a cent between the bid and ask prices, were suddenly dollars wide. At times, there was no market at all.

As if things weren't bad enough, the bottom then fell out of the crude oil market. We were already at Defcon-1 dealing with natural gas, and suddenly another one of our positions was moving sharply against us. This just became a two-front war.

Gas rallying through the roof and crude oil tanking simultaneously? What the heck was going on?

If traders knew the reason why natural gas was up 50 percent, the prices of our short call-options would have increased dramatically, but they would still have been trading. In that scenario, I would have bought them back at a premium to where I had sold them and lived to fight another day. I would have taken a substantial loss on the trade, but I wouldn't have lost the firm. Unfortunately, that is not the scenario we were in.

Winning trades take care of themselves. It's how we respond to the losers that determines success in the long run. I knew this. Throughout my career I had been aggressive about cutting losses early and often.

This time, the market wouldn't let me out.

CHAPTER 3

WHEN IT RAINS IT POURS

MONDAY, NOVEMBER 19, 2018

The video went viral over the weekend. What had been intended as a private message for 290 clients now has a million views all over the world. By Sunday night, the same prestigious media outlets that cited me as a top expert on commodity markets for the past two decades are showcasing the video and giving their hindsight critiques.

The Wall Street Journal compared me to Bernie Madoff. The Tampa Bay Times referred to me as a 'laughingstock' and, for some reason, printed details revealing the location of our home. The list goes on.

Krista and I are too embarrassed to show our faces in public. We just want to get on the *KR* and sail somewhere far away. But I can't leave, at least not yet.

I'm still captain of the *OS*, and my duty is to go down with the ship. I owe one-on-one conversations to a lot of clients. Those are going to be tough. I also have an office full of employees who have just been put through the wringer. They're probably wondering how much longer they will continue to receive a paycheck.

I have the best employees in the world. It's an all-star team that took years to assemble, and the thought of letting them go is heartbreaking. I spend Monday with them, figuring out what our next steps will be. There are lots of questions, answers, tears, and hugs exchanged. More questions than answers.

Everyone on staff will be paid at least through the end of the year. A core group is being kept in place indefinitely, to help deal with the headaches which are sure to follow. Client services, regulatory investigations, and potential litigation will be our priority for the next six months. After that, I hope, we will reopen for business.

It's been a long day following a very long week. I am mentally and physically exhausted. After dinner, Krista and I do our best to avoid watching the news and go to bed at a reasonable hour for the first time in a while. I fall asleep the moment my head hits the pillow.

Bang…bang…bang

Someone is pounding on our front door. The clock on my phone reads 12:05 a.m.

Not knowing what to think, we remain quiet and keep the lights off as I prepare for a potential home invasion. Krista half-jokingly whispers, "I told you we needed a panic room."

We live in a gated community with a 24-hour guard posted at the only entrance. Unannounced guests are never allowed in, let alone at midnight.

Could it be one of our neighbors? Is it security?
Why would they knock so aggressively?

After banging on the door a few more times and yelling something that we couldn't hear clearly, the unidentified person lingers on our doorstep and in our driveway for several minutes before abruptly leaving. Staying away from the windows, we fail to get a good look at them or their vehicle.

Krista asks if we should call the police.

"And tell them what? That someone knocked on our door? I don't need to give the internet another excuse to write a story about me."

Perhaps I'm being paranoid.
All the criticism is getting to me.

We don't know whether the perpetrator will return, and we aren't taking any chances. Quickly and quietly, we pack overnight bags, make our way to the garage, get in my car and slip out of the house in a hurry.

Not sure where to go, we stop at a well-lit gas station just to catch our breath and figure out a gameplan. I go to top-off my gas tank, but the pump rejects my debit card. The machine is probably offline. I think nothing of it.

We both need sleep, but don't want to go back home. Passing by an Embassy Suites, we pull in to get a room for the night. I hand the clerk my card and it fails to go through, again. We try another card and that one gets declined too. My accounts are frozen.

I offer cash and provide my driver's license, but the hotel only accepts cards. It's now almost 2:00 a.m. I explain that we will go to the bank first thing in the morning to straighten this out. The manager says his hands are tied, but he is tapping away at the computer behind the front desk, apparently trying to find some kind of solution to help us out.

The manager sees something on the screen that causes his facial expression to change. He glances up at me and says, "Wow. Looks like you had a rough week, Mr. Cordier," pronouncing it, 'Cor-deer'.

I didn't realize it, but he had been Googling my name while we were talking. He must have seen the long list of derogatory headlines and links to the viral apology video which are accompanied by a thumbnail photo of me sitting behind my desk looking devastated.

That dang video is going to haunt me
for the rest of my life.

Without further discussion, the hotel manager slides two room keys across the desk and says we can sort out the payment tomorrow. He's being sympathetic, or perhaps merciful. This is the first time since this ordeal began that a stranger is showing me anything but contempt. The Maserati parked out front and the Rolex on my wrist tell him that we're probably good for the $185.

We sleep past 8:00 a.m., and I wake up to dozens of unread text messages. Some are from friends and family sending kind words of encouragement. Many are from journalists asking for comment. Several are from Rosemary, who was busy scheduling my upcoming calls with clients. One is from Michael, Option-Sellers' director of research and marketing, telling me that he has reporters knocking on the windows of his house.

And one from Matthew, the head of my trade execution desk, sent at 7:15 a.m. It appears to be a photo of a business card, and the message reads: "This guy just showed up at my door asking questions."

Matt must be getting harassed by reporters, too.
Sorry, no time to look at that now.

Krista and I drive to Bank of America. I call ahead to let the branch manager, Michelle, know that we're coming in. It's a small branch in a small town. They don't handle many high net worth accounts. Two months ago, when I requested a seven-figure transfer to purchase *The Krista Renee*, Michelle requested to take a photo with me. I didn't mind, but it was a little strange.

Today, she's not nearly as friendly. She isn't providing us with much information, but it's clear our relationship has changed. She informs me that I have been "de-banked", and nobody at Bank of America can tell me why.

The account was not seized by the government but closed by the bank itself. The funds in the account are now in limbo. Without warning or explanation, the nest egg I've been building since I was a teenager has become totally inaccessible.

This can't be a coincidence. It must have something to do with the catastrophic events of last week, but I don't know what the connection could possibly be. Things just keep going from bad to worse.

As we're walking out of the bank, I take out my phone to call my lawyer, Henry Becker. I leave him a message.

I see that I have a new voicemail from a local phone number and give it a listen.

"Hi James, this is Chuck down at the marina. Just wanted to let you know that I've had three different people stop by and ask which boat is yours. I told them I didn't know what they were talking about, or who you were. It's none of their business. Anyway, I just thought you should know. By the way... I heard the news about what happened. I hope you're doing alright. Give me a call if you need anything."

Then I start scrolling through my texts again, trying to get caught up.

What was that business card Matthew sent earlier?
Oh, there it is:

U.S. Department of Justice

Federal Bureau of Investigation

New York Field Office

CHAPTER 4

INTRINSIC VALUES

I was born and raised in Sturgeon Bay, Wisconsin, a small shipbuilding town located about halfway up the Door Peninsula separating Green Bay from Lake Michigan. My family has lived there for generations. My father, James Cordier Sr., grew up there during the Great Depression. As a child he performed music at the local pub in exchange for 25 cents and a pint of beer per night.

My father learned to survive at a young age and maintained that work ethic throughout his life. As a teenager, he went to work on the 800-foot freight vessels that sailed through our town and across Lake Michigan. The giant ships loaded with iron ore, timber, and other commodities looked surreal passing through the small Sturgeon Bay Canal. Shortly after marrying my mother, he retired from sea life to become a local policeman.

Most people from my parents' generation never dreamed of becoming wealthy. Success for them meant being able to put a roof over their family's heads and food on the table. By that metric, my parents were quite successful. We lived in a small house in a peaceful neighborhood with a yard and a basketball hoop in the driveway.

And I never missed a meal. My mother had a talent for stretching her dollar at the grocery store to put a delicious meat-and-potatoes dinner on the table every night. She often provided a sweet treat for us at the end of the meal, prepared from raspberries that she had canned the previous summer. It was simple, but to us it might as well have been bananas foster flambé.

Raising six kids on a cop's salary meant there wasn't much disposable income, though I still think we had it pretty good compared to most. With me being the youngest, my dad had softened up a bit by the time I came around, but he was still a strict disciplinarian. He had rules, and we followed them with no debate on the subject.

I'm not sure what you would call my father's value system — patriotism, Midwestern manners, blue collar work ethic, maritime law, lessons from the school of hard knocks… It was a combination of all those and more. Sometimes his rules appeared to conflict, and other times they complemented each other perfectly. They were universal values, centered on family, responsibility, hard work, merit, honesty, and respect for authority. But also, on enjoying life.

Though my father was not a religious man, my mother enrolled us in the parochial school at St. Joseph's Church, and Dad was more than happy to pay the small tuition. Mom and I said our prayers together every night. I did it primarily to make her happy, but also found great comfort in it. I didn't realize it at the time, but I was shaping my own personal value system which, years later, would help me stay on course as I navigated through life as a young man.

Like every other boy in Wisconsin, I was obsessed with becoming the next quarterback of the Green Bay Packers. In the sixth grade, however, I got distracted by a shiny object that would eventually sideline my lifelong dream of playing pro football.

During show-and-tell, a classmate brought in his collection of coins from around the world. Having never stepped foot outside Wisconsin, the concept of foreign currency was fascinating to me. He owned coins from places that I had only read about, like the Philippines, Norway, India, and Argentina. I was intrigued by the value of those tiny metal shekels, and it prompted me to start my own collection.

As a byproduct of learning about coins, I also learned about exchange rates and inflation. I found out that dimes, quarters, and half-dollars minted prior to 1965 contained real silver. At the time (mid 1970s), you would still sometimes get a silver vintage coin in your change from the grocery store.

I developed an ability to identify the distinct sound a silver coin made when it jingled in the cashier's drawer or customer's hand. When I bought a 25-cent piece of candy, I paid with a dollar bill and pointed out which three quarters I wanted back. It probably drove them nuts.

Before long, I was going to the local bank to obtain rolls of quarters. I opened them up, sifted through to find a silver coin or two, then rerolled them to trade back in. This worked for a while, with diminishing returns over time.

As that well ran dry, I began to purchase silver coins, ingots, and bars with every dollar I could get my hands on. The local jewelry store owner, Mert, sold those items on the side but he never seemed too enthused about it.

I worked a variety of jobs in order to feed my silver addiction. I shoveled snow in the winter, mowed lawns and picked cherries in the summer, and delivered newspapers all year round. This allowed me to become a regular customer at Mert's jewelry store.

Every time I entered the store, the brass bell above the door clanged. Old Mert looked up with a big smile on his face, hoping he was about to sell an expensive watch or necklace to a member of one of the wealthy merchant families in town. When he saw me, that smile quickly soured to an expression that said, "Oh great, the kid is back to haggle over silver again."

After school I picked up 30 copies of *The Door County Advocate* for my afternoon delivery route. The newspaper distributor always had day-old copies of *The Wall Street Journal* and other papers laying around, and they let me take one for free. I read every article pertaining to metal prices and began tracking the daily settlement price of silver on graph paper which I pinned up on the wall of my bedroom.

Whenever I had the opportunity, I hitched a ride down to Green Bay with one of my parents or older siblings. There was a proper coin store downtown, run by a man named Mike who actually enjoyed talking coins and precious metal prices. There were times when I hung around that shop for more than an hour while my father visited other stores downtown. Mike introduced me to a publication called Numismatic News, which was all about coin collecting. Needless to say, I subscribed.

I didn't completely give up on football. I made quarterback of my high school team and led them to a 1-7 record. At least we won homecoming!

It was not generally expected that my siblings or I would attend college. It was simply too expensive. Most of the men in our town went to work at the shipyard after high school, and they made a pretty good living.

Nonetheless, my older brother Patrick was determined to find a way to attend university. I was two years younger, and accustomed to following his lead, so I paid close attention to his every move.

With interest rates near 20%, student loans were out of the question. Patrick worked two jobs to pay tuition at the University of Wisconsin Oshkosh. I didn't know whether it was because he had no money left over for food, or because the dining hall couldn't compare to our mom's homecooked meals, but Patrick didn't seem to eat much at school. During his first semester, he came home for Thanksgiving looking rather gaunt, and I began to question the wisdom of his decision.

That was when I started to seriously consider other options for myself- to decide what kind of life I wanted to live. It seems most of the people who grow up in Door County end up remaining there for life. I can't blame them, as it is the most beautiful place on earth.

I felt compelled to take a different path. Those massive ships that passed through our small town signified the world of opportunities that awaited. My parents sacrificed to provide for their children, making it possible for us to pursue our dreams. I owed it to them to make sure I pursued mine.

CHAPTER 5

RUNNING AGROUND

TUESDAY, NOVEMBER 20TH, 2018

10:00 AM

"The FBI came to your house?" I ask Matthew over the phone as Krista and I are getting in my car leaving the bank.

"Yeah, two of them. They pounded on my door at 7:00 a.m. I hadn't even had my coffee yet."

"Why? What did they want?"

I'm more confused than worried.

"At first, they asked a bunch of pointless questions about OS. Basic stuff that they would have easily been able to find in our NFA filings. 'How many clients? What commodities do we trade? Who clears our trades?' Stuff like that. They didn't seem to understand the subject matter."

"That doesn't make any sense. Why would the FBI be doing that? That's not their job."

"Well, I think I eventually figured it out. After about 15 minutes of nonsense, they asked one last question which was totally out of left field. They wanted to know whether I knew anything about you buying an expensive boat."

Why is the FBI asking my employee about a boat
I bought for my wife?

"What did you tell them?"

"I laughed and said, '*That's* what this is about?'" Matthew is always direct, sometimes to a fault. He continues, "All of their initial questions seemed like a pretense just to ask about the yacht. My guess is that they saw a large purchase around the same time that a lot of money was lost and thought, 'maybe there's some funny business going on.' I figured they were trying to find out if you were taking the other side of our trades, or getting kickbacks from someone who did, or somehow laundering money through the trading accounts. Something like that. They're barking up the wrong tree, obviously."

"Where would they get that idea?" I wondered aloud.

"I think they were just fishing in the dark. Maybe a disgruntled client gave them an anonymous tip to get back at you? I have no clue. Anyway, I guaranteed them that you weren't doing anything like that. I told them I was the one who executed the transactions. If you had been doing anything abnormal, like trying to steer a trade toward a specific counterparty, I would have known about it. I would have had to be involved. So, I know for a fact that you weren't... It's probably not what a lawyer would have advised me to say, but it's true. I figured I'd save them the wild goose chase."

I don't know how to process any of this.

"Okay. Is there anything else I should know?"

"Well, it's funny. The building I live in requires a fob to get in, and nobody was working behind the front desk at that hour. They must have lurked around and snuck in the door after one of my neighbors walked out. Seems like strange behavior for the FBI. That's why I checked their credentials. Their ID seemed legit, but what do I know? Also, did you notice that they were from the New York Field Office? You'd think they would send someone local."

That doesn't seem "funny" at all to me. My heart is racing.

"I gotta go, Matthew. I'm getting a call from Henry."

Henry Becker is an expert in the law governing the commodity futures industry. He handles my contracts and routine legal matters. He's a great lawyer, and just as importantly I trust him, but I'm not sure whether he has the right experience to deal with an FBI investigation. Especially since we still don't know why they're investigating.

Henry and I have been on the phone several times in the past few days, and he's been advising me on how best to deal with the aftermath of the trading losses. I expect him to be shocked when I tell him about the FBI inquiry.

"Hmm, that's odd," is his initial response. He sounds a bit cavalier about it.

"What should we do, Henry? Should we call the number on the card? Do I need to hire a criminal attorney?"

"That depends. Are you a criminal?"

He's being facetious, but I'm in no mood for it.

"Why does it seem like you're not taking this seriously? It's the FBI. You're supposed to be my lawyer. This is troubling."

Henry responds, matter of fact, "I think Matthew's assumption was probably right. Someone at the FBI saw your story in the news, did a cursory investigation on the internet, saw a million-dollar boat purchase, and decided to take a shot in the dark. Let them waste time looking into it."

"Several news outlets want to interview me about what happened. Maybe I should go on and clear my name before this FBI thing goes any further. Before it goes public."

"That's a terrible idea," Henry said, "Anything you say to the press will be twisted around, taken out of context, and used against you in litigation. Just sit tight. In six months, you'll reopen the firm, and you can take advantage of the free publicity then."

"I'm sure you're right, but it's hard to remain silent while my name is dragged through the mud."

Henry was always right. He had advised me not to put out that video in the first place. But I'm still worried. Being investigated by the federal government is unnerving- perhaps even more so when you've done nothing illegal.

"Oh, and there's another thing," I continue, "Bank of America froze all of my money and is refusing to tell me why."

"Okay, now that's a problem." Henry finally sounds as concerned as I am. "Perhaps it would be a good idea to bring in someone who specializes in these matters."

CHAPTER 6

SILVER RULE

A round the same time that I bought my first silver coin, back in 1973, two brothers in Texas commenced with a similar plan. Herbert and Bunker Hunt, oilmen by trade and gamblers by reputation, were concerned that their vast fortunes were being eroded by rampant inflation. In response, they bought 50 million ounces of silver in the form of exchange-traded commodity futures.

It was an astonishingly large position to begin with, and then they did something truly extraordinary. They took physical delivery of the metal. Speculators almost always close their futures contracts prior to settlement in order to avoid the burdensome cost of transportation and storage.

The Hunts' silver weighed over three million pounds. It had to be picked up by a fleet of armored cars at the COMEX (the exchange on which silver futures are listed) warehouse vault. From there it was taken to the airport, loaded onto chartered jumbo jets, and flown to Switzerland for safekeeping. It was a bold move, to say the least.

Six years later, in the summer of 1979, I was about to enter my senior year of high school. I had been accumulating and charting the price of silver for so long that the faded sheets of graph paper pinned up next to one another spanned an entire wall of my small bedroom. The other three walls were reserved for posters of Bart Starr, Farah Fawcett, and the Ramones.

I read every book I could find on fundamental and technical analysis and studied my *Wall Street Journal* every night. I worked and saved money for months at a time, until the chart on my wall indicated that it was a good time to buy, and then I loaded up.

There were times when my charts indicated the price of silver was going to pull back in the near term. I was always tempted to sell my holdings, so that I could buy it all back later at a lower price. Unfortunately, the haircut of 50 cents per ounce at Mert's jewelry store made that type of high frequency trading unprofitable.

For that, I would have needed a commodity futures trading account. That would've allowed me to trade in and out of silver as frequently as I wanted at the going market price – for a small commission instead of the massive haircut. Unfortunately, at the age of 17 I was not yet old enough to do that.

Undeterred and bullish on the long-term value of silver, I kept adding to my physical collection whenever I saw an opportunity.

During the six years since Herbert and Bunker Hunt's initial purchase, they had also continued opportunistically adding to their position. In August 1979, I read they were teaming up with members of the Saudi royal family to acquire an additional block of 40 million ounces worth of silver futures. The expectation was for them to take delivery once again. If they were to follow through on their plan, the Hunt brothers would soon control nearly 10% of the world's known silver supply.

There was growing concern that COMEX did not hold sufficient physical reserves to cover such a large obligation. If true, the exchange would be forced to purchase more bullion on the open market. By September, those fears caused the price of silver to double from $8 to $16 per ounce. That was just the beginning.

In December, the price of silver surpassed $20 per ounce. The Commodity Futures Trading Commission (CFTC) was expected to adopt new rules that would severely restrict the Hunts' ability to continue cornering the silver market. The additional rules were to be implemented in March of 1980, giving Herb and Bunker about three months to liquidate the vast majority of their position.

Remaining true to their gambler reputation, the Hunts attempted to call the CFTC's bluff. Instead of selling their holdings, they bought even more futures contracts, bringing their combined stake in silver to more than 200 million ounces. Their strategy worked for a while, driving the price above $30 in the first week of January 1980. This brought the total value of their position to more than seven billion dollars, on paper.

In response, COMEX passed a measure known as Silver Rule 7, tightening margin restrictions in an attempt to curtail silver buying.

I owned several hundred ounces by that point, and it was starting to look like a good time to take a little off the table. I didn't know how to predict when the price squeeze might reach its peak. I didn't even have an educated guess.

I had been relying predominantly on technical indicators to make my decisions, but chart analytics become unreliable during parabolic market moves. There was no playbook, I would have to rely on my judgement.

I asked my father what I should do. His advice, much like his booming baritone voice, could cut straight through any amount of noise. He had no opinion on the price of silver but understood the situation perfectly when he said, "Just don't be greedy, son."

The market price of silver was more than triple my cost basis. That meant if I sold a third of my collection, I stood to recoup every dollar I had ever invested in silver and would still own most of it free and clear. That plan made a lot of sense to me at the time.

I carefully counted and weighed the exact amount of silver that I wanted to part with and drove to the jewelry store to cash in on the biggest payday of my life. With so much recent price volatility, I anticipated the transaction fee might increase from 50 cents per ounce to perhaps one dollar. That would have been acceptable given the circumstances.

To my disappointment, Mert offered me barely half of the current market rate. He claimed that "real world" demand was not compatible with the price on the exchange. Mert was low-balling me because he didn't have any competition in town. That was unacceptable. I stormed out, unwilling to give away the lion's share of my profit to a middleman.

When the outrage wore off, I was overcome with fear that the price of silver would collapse before I had a chance to sell. That fear eradicated any lingering doubt as to whether selling was the right decision. I knew that I had a rare opportunity on my hands, and the clock was ticking.

I had faith that Mike's Coin Shop in Green Bay would be willing to pay a fair price based on that day's settlement price, but I had to give him enough time to withdraw cash before the bank closed at 3:00 p.m. I drove my 1973 Gran Torino an hour south, white-knuckling the steering wheel on snow covered roads, and barely making it in time.

Mike said that demand for physical bullion actually *exceeded* the price reflected on the exchange. He was an honest businessman who knew that he would be able to turn a quick profit of a buck or two per ounce. That seemed fair to both of us, so he closed the shop while we walked across the street to the bank. I went home with a wad of cash in my pocket wondering whether I should have sold more.

The next day, a man called our house and asked to speak with Jim Cordier. My father (Jim Sr.) listened silently for a moment with an increasingly furrowed brow, then held the olive green receiver of the rotary phone out toward me.

"I think it's for you," he said.

CHAPTER 7

BIG GUNS FROM THE BIG APPLE

January 2019

I scheduled a meeting with a high-powered New York law firm, Kasowitz Benson Torres LLP, that handles this sort of thing regularly. They didn't want to discuss the matter on the phone, preferring that I come up to New York and meet in person. I flew up from Tampa with my wife, and Henry Becker flew in from Chicago to join us.

Waiting in the Kasowitz reception area, I already feel reassured. It's a modern office in Midtown Manhattan with floor to ceiling windows, a stone's throw from Wall Street. The place is impeccably decorated, as one would expect considering their retainer and hourly rate. They are highly professional and have an air of competence. I'm confident that we have found the right guys for the job.

We're shown to a glass conference room where I sit down on one side of a long table, with Henry and Krista to my left and right. Our Pomeranian, Abigail, is in her carrier bag on the chair next to Krista. Across the table sit Marc Kasowitz and several members of his team. Following a brief exchange of small talk and pleasantries, they get right down to business.

"Alright, Mr. Cordier," begins one of the Kasowitz staffers. "Thank you for being here in person. You have retained Kasowitz Benson Torres as your attorneys on this matter, and everything you tell us will be protected by attorney-client privilege... This conference room is soundproof and has no recording devices."

"You're welcome," I reply, not quite knowing where to start. "I like meeting face-to-face too. I'm old fashioned like that."

I provide a quick recap of the events of the last few months while they take notes — the trading blow up, the FBI visit, the de-banking. When I finish, they provide an overview of how they would handle the case. About thirty minutes had passed when Krista leaves the room to tend to Abigail. The staffers leave with her. It's now just Marc, Henry, and myself in the room.

"In order to represent you properly, it is imperative that you be completely honest with me." Clasping his hands together in front of his chin, Marc takes on a more serious and deliberate tone. "I need to know about any potential vulnerabilities. So, tell me about the skeletons in your closet... Do you have any hidden assets? Secret trading accounts? Swiss or Caribbean bank accounts? Crypto wallet? Have you bought or sold any fine art? Received kickbacks related to OptionSellers business? Do you have any criminal associates? Drug, alcohol, or gambling problems? Mistresses? Burner phones?" He continues listing items in this manner.

"I don't have any of those things. I'm a flippin' Boy Scout… See, I rarely even use swear words." I'm trying to add some levity, but it's also true.

Marc asks whether I have received warnings or disciplinary action pertaining to our use of client funds or portfolio management.

I tell him that I didn't even have access to client funds — those are held by the futures clearing merchant. I had authority to place option trades in their account, but we're not custodians of the money. I couldn't pull cash from those accounts if I wanted to. As for portfolio management, I'm an open book. *Literally, I wrote a book about it.*

Every time market regulators audited our records — which is standard in my industry — we bent over backwards to give them everything they needed. The NFA (National Futures Association) recently completed just such a review. It took issue with a piece of marketing material because we failed to include a boilerplate disclaimer at the bottom, but nothing about our trading strategy or risk profile.

Just a few months ago, I invited several members of the risk department from FC Stone, our Futures Clearing Merchant, down to Florida to meet in person. We didn't have any specific issues to address, but I wanted to make sure we were operating well within its boundaries. I told them if there's ever the slightest concern with our portfolio, they could call me directly and I would make the necessary adjustments.

The risk management team was confused by that, and one of them hesitantly pointed out, "Honestly, James, before you invited us down here, I didn't even know who you were. Which is weird because you're one of our biggest CTA clients, and I'm the guy that issues the margin calls. Your name has never come across my desk."

All of our client accounts have been held at FC Stone for the last five years or so. Until last November's catastrophic event in natural gas, none of them had ever received a margin call. That is exceedingly rare, especially for a firm that exclusively sells options.

About a year ago, the CME (Chicago Mercantile Exchange) risk monitors reached out because our precious metals position had grown to account for a high percentage of the open interest in a particular contract month. It didn't necessarily have a problem with that, but it was showing up on the radar.

Many trading firms would have disregarded that type of notice, as there was no action required. I immediately scheduled a phone call with the CME to explain our risk procedures. I also offered to reduce the position if preferred.

I was not Bunker Hunt. I went beyond playing by the rules. I called the regulators on myself, just to make sure there wasn't even a whiff of impropriety. My father was a police officer, I learned to play by the rules at an early age. Now I'm a pariah that's being investigated by the FBI.

"What exactly happened during that second week of November?" Marc asks again, being more specific with his question.

"We had a short position in natural gas calls. It was one of our larger positions, comprising maybe 20% of our option portfolio and 10% of total equity allocation. Nothing out of the ordinary. The market moved against us to a point where it reached our internal risk threshold. I attempted to close out of the position but couldn't get the trades filled. A few other commodities broke in the wrong direction at the same time, and over the course of three trading days we lost everything. More than everything... by the time we were able to get out, the net liquidation value had gone into the red. That's the whole story."

Marc takes a long pause to consider everything I just told him. He removes his glasses and places them on the table, shifts in his chair, and lets out a slow audible exhalation. Then he gives me a quizzical look and asks,

"Are you telling me this is all over a bad trade?"

"Yes! That's all there is to it. To be fair, it was a really bad trade. It lost a lot of money." I continue, "I failed to do what I set out to do — to protect my client's capital. I own that, and I feel sick about what transpired. But I was acting in good faith. I was trying to generate profits using the same general trading strategy and risk parameters that I told them I would be using, the same ones I'd been using for years, the ones I had published books

41

about. There was nothing unethical, let alone illegal, about any of it."

Marc Kasowitz looked at me as if to say, "Then why the hell do you need us?"

A few minutes later, after Krista reentered the room, Marc said: "We will get this straightened out for you, but it's going to take some time. If what you've told me is true, it doesn't seem like you have much to be worried about in terms of criminal or civil penalties. Financially, the legal fees are going to take a toll. There will likely be lawsuits and arbitrations and possibly a deeper investigation by the regulatory agencies. Those are punishments in and of themselves."

He paused and looked at both of us.

"On a personal level, I just want to warn both of you to hold on tight. It's going to be a rough year ahead. In cases like this, the marriage almost never survives."

CHAPTER 8

PLAYING WITH CHAINSAWS

STURGEON BAY, WI
JANUARY 1980

I took the telephone receiver from my father's hand and stretched the cord from the kitchen to my bedroom so I could have some privacy. It was Mike, the coin dealer from Green Bay, he had looked my name up in the phone book. The price of silver bullion increased yet again, and he had a customer who was eager to buy. The next morning, I drove back down and sold almost every piece of silver that I owned for about $33 per ounce. I kept only a few rare coins that had sentimental value.

Within days, the price of silver futures on the COMEX reached a brief intraday high above $50 per ounce, which marked the height of the panic.

Not long after that, the regulators won their showdown with the Hunts, forcing them to liquidate their position. Within just a few weeks, the price of silver fell back down to about $12. Herb and Bunker Hunt were barred from trading commodity futures, and eventually forced to file for bankruptcy.

I fared much better. I made a killing on the trade, and I learned a valuable lesson about taking profits. One of the generally accepted rules of trading is to cut losses and let winning trades run, but the devil is in the details. Sometimes, when a market is highly volatile or appears to be behaving irrationally, you must cash out or risk giving back all the gains. There are exceptions to almost every rule.

Flush with cash, I now had the means to attend college if I truly wanted to. I had been recruited by a few Division-3 schools to play football. I also considered attempting to walk-on at the University of Wisconsin, with hopes of earning a scholarship — but that was beyond a long shot.

The decision tormented me. I was determined to become a professional commodity trader and assumed I would need a college degree to get my foot in the door. On the other hand, I already was a commodity trader of sorts, and I didn't want to spend all my capital on tuition.

I decided to work odd jobs while speculating on silver until I had more money saved up, then I would revisit the issue. By then I was over eighteen and had opened a futures trading account with Northwest Commodities.

After visiting friends at the University of Wisconsin in Madison, I realized that I wanted to be near that social scene. I knew that in order to meet girls, I would have to get out of my parents' house in Sturgeon Bay. I had a decent singing voice, and rudimentary guitar skills, so I joined a punk rock band with my friend Tony from high school.

The band leader, Brian, was a year or two older and also from Sturgeon Bay. Unlike the rest of us, he was a real musician. Brian taught Tony and me how to play well enough to perform in front of an audience.

We rounded out the lineup with Tim the drummer. Tim was in his mid-20s and a bit of a loose cannon. He had been a member of several similar bands in the past and seemed to know his way around the business.

We called ourselves "The Chainsaws" and dressed the part of social misfits.

The four of us rented a house together in Madison and spent several hours a day practicing. In between rehearsing covers of anti-establishment anthems, I sat on my amplifier and read the *Wall Street Journal*. The irony was lost on me at the time.

Tim expressed grand delusions about becoming famous, but I never expected that. I loved music, but commodity trading was the only profession I was interested in.

My time in Madison was transformational. I may have moved there for the music and the girls, but I stayed for the education.

In those days, before digital identification cards, it was easy for a college-aged kid to walk into the university library. I couldn't check out any books, but I could stay there all day and read anything I wanted. So that's what I did.

The band had a few successful gigs at local bars and frat parties. At our peak we were pulling in $150 per show, split four ways. Our most high-profile performance was in front of more than a thousand people at a summer festival back in Sturgeon Bay.

We were opening for a country-western group called The Johnsons, who were quite popular in the region. Their fan base didn't care for our sound or our appearance, so we played to a chorus of boos. After a few songs, the crowd began to throw empty beer cans toward the stage. We thought it was cool, and it bolstered our rebel image.

Six months after moving into the house in Madison, Tim was struggling to come up with his share of the rent on time. The utilities were under his name, and so the electricity had been shut off. The gas and water were next. What's worse is that his girlfriend had moved into the house, too.

I suggested that we all get jobs, but Tim was 'too punk rock' for that. He expressed a particular aversion to the idea of wearing a suit and tie, supposedly because uniformity stifles creativity. That was when I realized we were dressed exactly the same as every other punk band in the world. Perhaps we weren't as rebellious as we thought.

The last straw was when Tim suggested that I dip into my savings to cover his share of expenses for a while, promising to pay me back when we signed our first big record contract. We were never going to get a record deal, and I think we all knew that. The writing was on the wall that it was time to move on. It had been fun pretending to be a rockstar for a while, but it wasn't really me. I just had to figure out what to do next.

Around the same time that The Chainsaws were breaking up, I was having a conversation with my broker at Northwest Commodities, Terry Winter. I was by far his youngest client with a self-directed trading account, which must have piqued his interest. Unbeknownst to me, he had been closely observing my trading activity for months.

Terry asked a lot of questions about how I made my trading decisions. I assumed that he was trying to verify whether I was qualified to trade my own account, so I tried to impress him. I told him about how I had followed the market since middle school, listed all the books I had read on commodities, told him that I read the Journal every day, and how I had cashed in on silver. Terry invited me down to Chicago to meet him in person.

A few days later, I was treated to the quintessential Chicago experience — a tour of the Board of Trade, followed by an afternoon game at Wrigley Field and a steak dinner. If I had any remaining doubts about my chosen career prior to that trip, they disappeared the moment I laid eyes on the trading floor.

Terry walked across the enormous grain room like he owned the place – cracking jokes with floor brokers and pit traders along the way. Many of them relied on Terry for business, as he typically called his orders in from an office several floors above. Terry was at least six-feet tall, but he was below average height on the trading floor where everyone seemed to be a giant. It was hard to tell exactly how tall anyone was down there, as we were all standing ankle-deep in scraps of paper — discarded trade tickets, price sheets, and miscellaneous refuse. Everyone else on the floor was wearing threadbare trading vests and faded black jeans. Terry had on a blue pinstriped suit and red "power tie." I didn't know what a power tie was, but I was impressed.

It was exhilarating to see grown men scream and yell, argue, fight, and put their money where their mouths were. It was raw, uncensored, and unlike any other job I could imagine — a primal representation of capitalism. It was the coolest thing I had ever seen.

We left for the game an hour before the market closed. As our taxi drove north on Lakeshore Drive, I asked Terry how the market had been treating him lately. He said it was treating *him* great, but his clients were getting smoked. I didn't understand what he meant by that, but I nodded as if I did.

The Cubs were playing the Cardinals, so even though it was 1:00 p.m. on a weekday, Wrigley Field was packed. Terry and I spoke casually about commodities and had a few beers during the game. At one point I referred to the profit I had made in silver the previous year as a windfall, and he immediately corrected me.

Terry kindly pointed out that I had put in the work every day for years and sacrificed and saved. Yes, there was plenty of luck involved, but I had put myself in a position to capitalize on that luck. I never thought of all my research and charting as work. It was just something I had done for fun, a hobby. Shoveling snow was work.

After the game, we took a cab back downtown for dinner at a fine steakhouse (I can't remember which one). There were plenty of tables available, but Terry suggested that we belly up to the bar. The bartender asked if he wanted 'the usual' and Terry said, "Yup, and the same for the kid," gesturing toward me. A few minutes later we each had a martini sitting in front of us.

By the end of the meal, we had consumed two T-bone steaks and four martinis between us — though I only had one of each. I probably spilled more than I drank, as I wasn't accustomed to handling a martini glass. As we parted ways on the sidewalk out front, Terry offered me a job as an associate commodity broker. I was totally caught off guard by that, but immediately agreed to move to Chicago and start in two weeks.

CHAPTER 9

BEANS IN THE TEENS

With 14 days to prepare for the new job in Chicago, I gave myself a crash course in the grain markets. I wouldn't just be analyzing silver anymore, as the firm's clients mostly traded soybeans, wheat, and corn.

Having grown up among cornfields, dairy farms, and orchards, I possessed a basic knowledge of agriculture. It's important to understand the physical properties of a commodity to understand its financial properties. Technical analysis can only take you so far.

After saying goodbye to friends and family around Wisconsin, I loaded all my worldly possessions into my old Gran Torino and drove 4.5 hours south to start my new life in the Windy City, the epicenter of commodity trading.

The Chicago Board of Trade was established in 1848 to standard-ize and regulate agricultural product markets. Forward contracts enabled farmers and ranchers to receive more predictable prices for their grain and livestock. This provided financial security which allowed them to reinvest in the following year's crop — thus laying the groundwork for the Midwest and Great Plains to become the breadbasket of America and the world.

I stayed on a friend's sofa on the far north side of the city and took the Red Line downtown first thing Monday morning. It was the height of summer, and already hot outside. I was wearing a new suit I had bought for $200 at Marshall Fields because I thought it looked like the one Terry had worn. I was trying desperately not to look like a small-town hayseed that just blew into the big city.

The Chicago Board of Trade Building is an architectural landmark, regarded as one of the great representations of Art Deco design. Walking down LaSalle Street before the market opened, I passed a group of traders smoking cigarettes out front. One pointed at me and said, "This kid looks like he's wearing his father's suit."

I didn't know why that was an insult, but it clearly was. I tried not to let it rattle me as I entered the building and took the elevator up to the Northwest Commodities offices. I informed the receptionist behind the front desk that I was there to report to Terry Winter. In a monotone voice and without looking up, she informed me that Mr. Winter was no longer with the firm.

During the intervening two weeks since I had been promised the job, the man who hired me had gotten himself fired.

"I'm sorry to hear that," I offered, not knowing what to say. "How will that impact my employment?"

"It precludes it," she said.

And just like that, I was back to being an amateur. Worse yet, I had to go back to Wisconsin and face all the people I had just said goodbye to a few days earlier. I was devastated, but it didn't last long.

On the drive home I thought about what my father would say, "Life is tough… Adversity is just an opportunity to grow stronger… I told you that trading commodities isn't a real job…" Not all his advice was encouraging.

My father would have preferred that I return to Sturgeon Bay and work at the boatyard, but he knew I was intent on leaving. Deep down, he begrudgingly respected me for it.

I saw the silver lining almost immediately. Sure, I was disappointed, but I was also in a better position than I had been in prior to receiving the offer. Even though it hadn't happened, I had proven that it was possible to land a big-time job in Chicago. It was like hooking into a trophy fish and reeling it to within a few feet of the boat before losing it. The close call helped me realize that my goal was within reach and strengthened my resolve to achieve it.

From that point forward I considered myself a professional commodity trader, even though I had no office or business card. I knew that trading commodities would come to define not only my career, but also my entire life. Considering that I was still only 20 years old, I thought I was doing alright.

I was armed with newly acquired knowledge about grain and livestock, and a notebook full of trade ideas. I wasn't going to continue giving Northwest Commodities my business after that ordeal, so I moved my trading account to another Chicago firm, Heinold Commodities. Soon I was putting those ideas to work in the market, with positive results.

Friends and relatives heard about my success and opened their own futures accounts with the same broker I was using at Heinold. They made money piggybacking my trades, which was great!

I may not have been the world's foremost expert on agriculture, but I knew that crops needed water, and it hadn't rained in a while. The information was right there in the newspaper, but the so-called experts did not seem to believe it. I thought maybe they saw something I had missed, but I couldn't figure out what that might be. Ultimately, I had faith in my analysis and went long on soybeans early in the year.

Experienced commodity traders take their news with a grain of salt. The business section needs a story, and "all is well" does not sell newspapers. In their search for content, journalists ask farmers for their thoughts on the upcoming harvest. Typically, the seller of a commodity will agree with any narrative that drives up the price.

Every year farmers say that either there wasn't enough rain or there was too much, it was either too hot or too cold for their crops to thrive. You'll never hear them say that it's going to be a bumper crop until after they've sold their product. The result is that editorials about commodity prices generally err toward being overly bullish. Seasoned traders learn to read between the lines.

Luckily, in early 1983 I was not yet a seasoned soybean trader. When I read that a drought and ensuing heat wave had badly damaged the U.S. crop, I believed it. Being in the Midwest, I was able to drive out and look at the farmland myself to confirm. The soybeans sure looked dry and brittle to my untrained eye. Soon, the broader market took notice, and the price of beans started to rise.

As the soybean rally ramped into high gear, my broker — who for months had been dismissing the notion of a drought — started buying for all his clients. The herd mentality was aston-ishing, and savvy traders used it to their advantage.

Brokers who had no interest when the price was $6 per bushel were suddenly racing to buy at $8. Then some of them would sell at $9, seemingly without ever having an opinion on the crop itself.

"Beans in the teens" became a popular rallying cry among bullish traders who now anticipated soybeans topping $13 per bushel for the first time.

I witnessed firsthand the impact that the market can have on herd mentality, and vice versa. Understanding and predicting this phenomenon is crucial to success in trading; so much so that many speculators make a living on that one ability alone.

I cashed in big on soybeans that year, turning $6,000 into $35,000, and once again my broker took notice. Heinold was opening a new branch office in Milwaukee and hired me as a broker. This time, the job materialized, and some of the people who had been piggybacking my trades signed on to be my first clients.

At Heinold, I would be able to expand my portfolio beyond silver and grains, into livestock and energy. With the resources of a big firm, I would have access to more information. I envisioned the life of a commodity broker to entail reading endless stacks of research reports, speaking with investors and industry experts, and formulating a trading strategy. That was exactly what I wanted to do and now I would have the opportunity… or so I thought.

CHAPTER 10

FROZEN AND SQUEEZED

O nce I started working at Heinold, I was disheartened to find out that the day-to-day activities of a typical commodity broker were not what I imagined. I had hoped I would spend 90 percent of my time on research and analysis and 10 percent tending to clients, but that ratio was reversed. Most brokers spent nearly all their time cold-calling, and when it came to portfolio management, they just went along with whatever recommendations were being spoon-fed to them by the firm. Regardless of that, I was excited to be a licensed commodity broker.

Outside of the office, I found that although most people were familiar with the term, they didn't know what a commodity broker actually did. Acquaintances would ask me how their IBM stock was going to perform that year. "I have no idea," was my honest response, but often they seemed to suspect I was being coy.

I didn't know much about the stock market and honestly didn't care to. I never wanted to place my faith or money in the hands of executives whom I would never meet. What attracted me to physical commodities is that they were much larger in scope than any one person or corporation, so they were inherently less susceptible to manipulation. Commodities are not without their imperfections, but they are the closest thing to a meritocracy among securities markets.

The only downside of being a commodity broker was the obnoxious sales tactics that we were expected to employ. Most brokers were boastful, pushy, and sometimes dishonest in their efforts to sign up new clients. Once the account was funded, the goal shifted to convincing them to agree to trades without fully thinking it through. Brokers created a false sense of urgency, as if every trade was a once-in-a-lifetime opportunity. They intentionally used jargon that the customer didn't understand, making them feel foolish or insecure.

I had not signed up to be a telemarketer and refused to go along with that business model. I thought that if I could just deliver solid returns, the amount of assets I had under management would naturally grow — from the profits themselves, from additional deposits made by satisfied customers, and from new clients acquired by word of mouth.

Experienced brokers at the firm viewed this approach as naive, and for a while they seemed to be proven correct. I had precious few clients in the beginning. Regardless of the consequences, I was not going to sacrifice my integrity or long-term plans in order to pad the current month's commission check. That would have been short-sighted.

On more than one occasion I was called into the branch manager's office to answer for why I failed to sign up the requisite number of new clients that month. My defense of pointing to the success of my few existing clients' portfolios fell on deaf ears.

After a while I learned to play the game just enough to stay off their radar, while remaining true to my values and long-term career plans. I still ended up spending half my energy in those early years on various forms of client acquisition, but I went about it my own way.

The film *Trading Places* was released in the summer of 1983. It's a hilarious comedy starring Eddie Murphy and Dan Ackroyd as commodity brokers. It was a must-see for people in my industry and served as a reference when friends and family asked what I did for a living. Soon they stopped asking about IBM stock and started asking about pork bellies. A key plot point of the film involved devious speculators attempting to corner the market in frozen concentrated orange juice (FCOJ) futures by falsifying the annual USDA crop report.

As the year drew toward a close, people on the trading floor joked about the actual USDA crop report which was scheduled to be released in early January. I don't know whether the movie influenced trading activity, but there was certainly a lot of chatter about orange juice. Not very many brokers specialized in OJ, but everyone had something to say about it that year.

As FCOJ futures rallied in the fourth quarter, shorting them started to look like an attractive trade. The prevailing wisdom around the office stated that, since orange juice was not a necessity, there would be greater price sensitivity as compared to grains or livestock.

Suddenly everyone was an expert. The experts agreed that the rally was overblown, and it was due for a pullback. I don't recall if there was an actual directive from upper management to short orange juice, or if it was just another case of herd mentality, but the whole firm was on the same page.

The attitude was euphoric, as some of my colleagues who had spent no time studying the fundamentals were suddenly overcome with fear of missing out. I was still learning the ropes of the grain markets at the time, and didn't have any experience with orange juice, so I was reluctant to sell at first. I began reading up on the subject, but there was no time for even a crash course. I had to decide either to jump on the bandwagon or risk missing out on what the experienced brokers around me seemed to think was a no-brainer.

I was still new in the job and had very few clients. Already drawing unwanted attention within the firm for my proclivity to do things my way, I felt pressure to take part in the trade. I was conflicted and, ultimately, I waffled. I succumbed to groupthink by taking a small, short position for my clients. It didn't take long for that to backfire.

On Christmas Day, 1983, Florida suffered its worst frost in a century. At the time, the Sunshine State produced 60 percent of the orange juice consumed in the United States.

The trading floor in our office had a large mechanical board that displayed real-time futures prices. That was cutting-edge technology for the time. It made a loud "clack" sound every time the price changed. When the market was moving in the wrong direction, brokers would dread the sound of those clacks throughout the day, as each one meant another incremental loss of capital.

In the final week of 1983, the firm would hear just one depressing clack per day, as FCOJ went limit-up (the maximum amount that a commodity price is permitted to change in one day before trading is halted by the exchange). This occurred immediately upon the market-open every morning, letting every broker on the floor know that they would lose the maximum amount possible that day. It was not a happy New Year.

It was eye-opening to witness ostensibly savvy traders join the herd just in time to run off a cliff. Many of them were completely wiped out. The damage from that trade was such that Heinold shuttered its Milwaukee branch shortly thereafter, even though it had opened with great fanfare only a year earlier.

My clients took a loss on the trade but were spared from catastrophe due to the relatively small stake I had taken. I couldn't exactly pat myself on the back for that. It had not been a strategic decision that led me to scale down the trade. I survived the OJ squeeze based on indecision, fear, and a bit of luck.

It was a close call that taught me a valuable lesson. Heinold invited me to work out of their Chicago office but, having been disillusioned by the whole experience, I opted to remain independent for a while.

CHAPTER 11

SAFE HARBOR

Growing up in the Northern Midwest, I sometimes wondered about my family's origins in the region. With our French surname, I liked to think that we were descended from the 18th century fur traders who were among the first Europeans to explore the area. Perhaps we had roots in the timber business which thrived during the 19th century, clearing the landscape that resulted in the dairy pastures for which Wisconsin is now known.

Regardless of the specifics, it seemed likely that I had genealogical ties to sailors or commodity merchants of some sort. This was mere speculation on my part, because the family history I knew of only went as far back as the stories my father would recount from his childhood.

Only recently, while doing some background research for this book, did I discover that there was truth to my childhood fantasy of having ancestors in the Wisconsin timber and shipping business. It turns out that my great-grandfather, Eugene Cordier, had been a successful lumber merchant during the 19th century. He owned thousands of acres of timber and a small fleet of ships to carry it to market.

In 1893, one of those ships, *The Willard A Smith*, took on a load of lumber at Horseshoe Bay, just north of Sturgeon Bay. A storm was looming, so he decided to play it safe by remaining in the harbor until it passed. Better to be a day late than risk not making it at all.

Winds shifted overnight and battered the ship against the dock, smashing both to pieces. It sank in six feet of water. Despite playing it safe, the ship and its cargo were lost, but at least the crew was not on board at the time.

Eugene suffered an economic crash at some point in his life. It's unclear whether that shipwreck played a major role or not. All I know is that by the time my father was born in 1918, there was no family fortune nor acres of timber. The family endured difficult times, but ultimately persevered. Commodity trading has been in our bloodlines all along, we just lost it for a couple of generations.

James Cordier Sr. was 11 years old when the Great Depression began. His family had been comfortably middle class, but suddenly they were thrust to the brink of poverty. My father began working odd jobs to pitch in, most notably singing and performing music on his concertina at the local pub. When he returned home each night, he left the 25 cents he had earned in the chest pocket of his shirt, which he hung in the hall closet. The next day when he put that same shirt back on, the quarter was always gone. His mother took it to help pay the household expenses. He understood this implicitly, though they never spoke of it.

That type of hardship was typical for that generation, and he never complained about it. When he did speak of his childhood, it was usually to share what he thought were hilarious anecdotes, like the one about how his mother once got angry and hit him with a broom, breaking it in half. The punchline was that for the remainder of his childhood she swept their home using a broom that had a jagged, two-foot-long handle.

In winter, my father and his friends played on the frozen canal, holding races and pick-up hockey games. They all wore rusty hand-me-down skates, and hockey sticks were fashioned from scrap lumber. When my father got to high school and strapped on a legitimate pair of skates for the first time, he went on to win the state title in speedskating. According to his retelling of the story, he was so far ahead in the final lap of the championship that when his hat blew off, he was able to go back to retrieve it mid-race, and still won.

As a teenager, my father became a deck hand on one of the Great Lakes freight vessels, which were a centerpiece of the Sturgeon Bay economy. He eventually worked his way up to helmsmen, steering the ship while the captain tended to other responsibilities. In winter, while the lakes were frozen, he worked in the local shipyard repairing boats. By the time I was born, he had long since retired from the sea life to become a local police officer.

Though he had a steady full-time job, my father carried on the tradition of letting children pitch in to support the family finances. He would take my brothers and I on early-morning fishing trips, which I thoroughly enjoyed. I used to sleep in my fishing gear the night before to ensure that I would be ready to go when he woke us before first light. It was common for us to battle four-foot, rolling waves in our 16-foot boat.

I always thought this was just a fun family activity, until my brothers spoiled it by letting me know that we were invited along primarily to increase the number of lake trout Dad was allowed to take home. The bag limit was five fish per head, and we needed as many as we could get. Other family activities included gathering night crawlers after it rained, and recycling scrap metal into sinkers, both of which we sold to local fishermen.

With six kids, money was tight regardless of how many odd jobs we picked up. One year, I begged my parents for an official Bart Starr jersey every day for the entire football season. On Christmas morning, I eagerly unwrapped a plain white undershirt with the number 15 screen-printed onto it. Another year, I asked repeatedly for a BB gun and my father always shot back, "You're not getting a gun!" as if I had requested an AR-15.

Eventually I wised up and tugged on his heartstrings by asking for a guitar. His love of music softened him up, and that guitar was by far the greatest material gift that I received as a child.

The experiences of his hardscrabble youth had my father forever focused on diversifying his income streams, though I doubt he ever thought of it in those terms. It was ingrained in him, as was a blue-collar lifestyle, but underneath the rough exterior he had the soul of an artist. In addition to music, my father also wrote poetry and made impressive sketches of the boats he encountered on the lake as a young man.

Later in life, he turned those sketches into incredibly detailed wooden replicas. Dad spent hours on end in the garage, painstakingly carving each piece. Building model ships is a cottage industry in Door County, and my father was among the most prolific at it. He sold dozens of them to local businesses and museums. He was jokingly referred to as the third largest ship-builder in Sturgeon Bay, behind only Peterson Builders (supplier of U.S. Navy minesweepers) and Palmer Johnsons (maker of world-renowned mega yachts).

After retirement, my father regularly hosted a poker game with his friends out in the garage. Once in a while, a new player would join them and go all-in several times in the first few hands – which annoyed the other players. When everyone else folded, that person would have a self-satisfied smile on their face. Dad liked to say, "It works every time until the last time."

Sure enough, that player would be the first one out of the game after they went all-in and someone else had pocket aces. Eventually, they would either learn to play the game properly or they would stop showing up.

CHAPTER 12

IN-THE-BLACK MONDAY

Untrustworthy leaders tend to attract untrustworthy employees. Stockbrokers have always been accused of being greedy, but in the 1980s they began to openly boast about it. Gordon Gecko had a valid point when he said, "Greed is good," but there is a difference between greed and rational pursuit of self-interest. Greed implies an *irrational* desire for money, leading to dishonesty and unscrupulousness. When those characteristics are rewarded, they grow like cancer.

The culture of Wall Street during the 1980s was toxic. Insider trading, high-pressure sales, fraud, and failure to perform due diligence were perceived as commonplace. It was not unusual to see brokers blatantly lying or snorting cocaine at their desks while on the phone with clients. That type of behavior was more common among bond traders, which was another reason why I preferred commodities over purely paper assets.

As the government worked to rein in inflation, unintended consequences began to unfold. From junk bond scandals to the savings-and-loan crisis, people had reasons to question their faith in the financial system. In October 1987, investors began to notice the warning signs, and everyone simultaneously rushed for the exit.

During the immediate aftermath of Black Monday, headlines focused on the turmoil in equity and debt markets, where Americans held much of their retirement savings. It seemed, as it so often does, that there was no solid understanding of how the event would affect mainstream markets going forward.

There was no shortage of opinions in the media about the cause of the crash, however there was a dearth of actionable information. Analysis pertaining specifically to commodities was especially hard to find. This was when I first conceived of the Cordier Commodity Report, though it would be a few years before it manifested.

The impact that inflation and interest rates would have on commodity markets was, at its core, predictable. As the dollar strengthened, the relative value of commodities weakened, assuming everything else remained constant. I needed to know which factors were not remaining constant, and I was not finding that information in my usual trusted sources. I began to look elsewhere.

I pivoted my research to meteorology because unbiased data on the subject was readily available. Following the weather was nothing new for a commodity trader, but I was determined to get a deeper understanding. Rather than waiting for a drought or frost to occur and then be written about in the newspaper, I wanted to see them coming weeks in advance. While it's impossible to forecast these events with perfect accuracy, I was able to track their probability over time.

I checked the weather reports in Florida and Brazil daily, hoping to get a jump on the next orange freeze. I never cashed in on that intended goal, but my research into South America improved my perspective on grains and livestock and brought my attention to the coffee market.

Getting reliable weather updates from around the globe was challenging back then, but critical information could be found in my hometown Midwest newspaper. Another drought was unfolding in the nation's heartland, mimicking the scenario I had capitalized on five years earlier.

Once again, grains rallied hard, and I was on the correct side. I had a nice string of beginner's luck. Up until that point, the orange juice squeeze had been my only significant loss, and I never wanted to find myself in that position again.

I searched for flaws in my analysis and played devil's advocate with every position in my portfolio. I refused to let wishful thinking enter the decision-making process, which is no easy task. There were still plenty of losing trades along the way, but I had sound logic behind all of them. Identifying weak positions and cutting losses early became my obsession.

To excel at this, I needed access to the advanced economic, agricultural, and weather reports that big firms typically pay a lot of money for. Having just made a bit of a name for myself in the grain market, I was hired by a firm located in Milwaukee that focused on agriculture futures.

The owner of the firm, Richard, was a flashy guy who took a bit too much pride in his money. He flaunted his wealth to people who did not have as much, including his employees. He was not a malicious person, perhaps just a little insecure. It's good to meet people like that early in life, because they can serve as an example of how not to act once you've achieved success.

Richard was always nice to me. He seemed to be nice to everyone. However, like many people in his position, he had underlings that handled the unpleasant aspects of managing employees. His top henchman was Gary, the sales manager.

The downstream effect of poor leadership is poor culture. Many of the brokers were overly aggressive in their sales tactics, nobody performed fundamental analysis, and one guy openly referenced astrology charts as the basis for his trades. It was a commission-only job, so the owner was not interested in micromanaging. The upside was that I was able to work on my own strategies with little oversight.

My client book was small but growing steadily by word of mouth. Many of the older brokers relied on a handful of loyal clients who made the same exact seasonal trades year after year. Most of the other young guys were constantly repeating the same tired sales pitch to an endless revolving door of new customers.

The business model seemed to be centered on overpromising performance to bring in new clients, then losing them a few months later when the results inevitably underdelivered, then repeat. I wanted to keep my existing clients around for as long as possible, so I tried to set realistic expectations from the beginning.

I offered more to my clients by mixing new strategies with reliable seasonal trades. We explored opportunities in livestock, heating oil, gold, and gasoline to keep things interesting. By monitoring a broader range of markets, I naturally discovered a greater number of attractive trade opportunities.

Though my accounts seemed to be more active than others at the firm who only traded grains, I was making comparatively less in commissions each month. I tended not to diversify my portfolio as much back then, preferring to take larger positions in just one or two commodities at a time.

Richard applauded my work ethic, at first. He used it as an example when reprimanding some of my peers who, in his opinion, had gotten lazy. This didn't help me win any popularity contests around the office. The old-timers liked things the way they were and certainly did not want to hear, "You should be more like James."

My portfolio was buoyed by another string of beginner's luck in these new markets, at one point recording 13 winning trades in a row. I remember that number because an elated client had just pointed it out and thanked me moments before I was summoned to the office of the sales manager, Gary.

I assumed that I was in for a promotion, or at least an "atta boy." Instead, he told me that this was an Ag trading firm (meaning agricultural commodities, like corn and wheat) and that I needed to trade Ags. I pointed out my success in metals and energy, to no avail.

"The problem with metals," he told me, "is that nobody trades spreads. There is no such thing as new-crop and old-crop gold."

He was referring to a common practice in the Ag markets, where traders spread one contract against another. This could mean taking a long position in this month's wheat contract versus a short position in next month's wheat contract. It could be spreading soybean oil futures versus soybean meal futures. It could be spreading corn versus live cattle.

There could be good reasons for placing any of those trades, but Gary did not seem to be motivated by good reasons. In this case, it appeared to be all about maximizing commissions. Trading 100 spreads for a client paid twice as much commission as trading 100 outright futures contracts, and the margin requirements were often lower. This meant far more commissions generated per dollar of assets under management. It also meant commissions were likely to outweigh profits on the trade.

I didn't want to trade spreads. If I was bullish on wheat, I just wanted to buy the wheat futures outright. I don't think upper management had a problem with that, but Gary felt that my disregard for the norms of the firm had become a distraction to other brokers. If I wanted to stay there, I would have to fall in line.

Their position was understandable, but I was not interested in fitting in with their culture. We agreed to part ways at the end of the following month, giving me plenty of time to find a new firm where I could take my handful of clients with me. It was an unusually magnanimous arrangement, for which I was — and still am — grateful.

The next day, I received a call from Paul Georgy, the owner of Allendale Securities. Richard must have given him my name because I had yet to inform anybody that I was looking for a new employer. It was a unique interview in that it was relaxed and friendly. By the end of the conversation, he offered me a broker position with Allendale and promised that I would be allowed to continue developing unorthodox portfolio strategies – within reason.

I was skeptical because it seemed too good to be true. It reminded me a little bit of my first job interview with Terry Winter a decade earlier, but this had a different feeling. Paul wasn't trying to impress me; he didn't need to. He was sincere and open about his plans for the firm, as well as what my role would entail.

CHAPTER 13

CORDIER COMMODITY REPORT

A fter those first few disappointing experiences with other brokerage firms, Allendale turned out to be a breath of fresh air. Paul Georgy was a man of his word. He allowed me to run my own branch office in Milwaukee, encouraged me to develop new trading strategies, and provided me with all the resources necessary to do so.

For the first time in my young career, I had a boss whom I truly admired. Paul was friendly, hardworking, research-oriented, and focused on the best interests of his clients. He was a great role model and living proof that it was possible for an honest man to succeed in this business.

I began producing *Cordier's Commodity Report*, a free newsletter featuring my analysis of current market trends. I brought copies of them to every conference I attended. I passed them out to other branch managers when we had meetings at the home office. Nobody asked me to do this, and it provided me with no apparent benefit at the time. In fact, it was a point of derision, as some of my peers mocked the idea. I assume they viewed me as an apple-polisher.

The analysis was useful to investors and served as a jumping-off point for interesting conversations with colleagues. I hoped that eventually it would help bring in new clients, but I truly enjoyed discussing commodity markets with anyone that was interested, so the CCR was a labor of love.

Most of my analysis pertained to boring subjects, like inflation data or seasonal rainfall averages, so occasionally I would try to spice things up. I'd discuss more sensational topics to draw in readers, whether those topics impacted my portfolio or not. One prime example of this came from the lumber market.

More than 30 billion board-feet of lumber are produced and consumed in the United States each year. However, I have never found it to be an enticing commodity to speculate on because it was difficult to gain an edge over the market. Demand is dictated by the housing cycle, which generally moves in concert with the overall economy. As a result, bull or bear markets in lumber were often relentless.

Supply tends to be stable, or at least predictable. Unlike most agricultural commodities, trees take many years to develop and are quite robust. Seasonality is not much of a factor. Forest fires, blight, floods, and droughts are too localized to have a major market-wide impact, at least not in the manner one might expect. Lumber seemed impervious to major supply disruptions, which meant risk premiums were cheap.

Then, during the early 1990s, the plight of the spotted owl gained national attention. Environmentalists were pushing the government to protect the tree-dwelling birds by banning logging on public land. There was suddenly a distinct possibility of an extreme shock to the supply of lumber, as millions of acres of timber could potentially be removed from the queue with the stroke of a pen. As the story played out in the media, there was widespread speculation on future prices.

In commodity circles, boring old lumber suddenly became a hotly discussed topic. The increased attention, volatility, and risk premiums convinced a few intrepid speculators to begin trading it. Retail investors watched the spotted owl story on the evening news and wanted to pick a side, often biased by their political beliefs. Suddenly, everyone was an expert, and brokers were more than happy to accept their orders. It reminded me of the euphoria surrounding orange juice years earlier.

Even if I had been an expert on the lumber market, trading it at that point would have been speculating on whether Congress was going to pass legislation. I didn't trade lumber, and I actively discouraged a few clients from taking a stake in it, but I used the interest in the situation to my advantage.

By writing about the spotted owl, the Cordier Commodity Report gained in popularity. Because it was an unsolicited free publication, the only way to measure its readership was by how often people mentioned it to me in conversation. My analysis of the spotted owl controversy became the default topic whenever I engaged in small talk with colleagues.

It soon spread to other commodities that I wrote about. After a while it became clear that other brokers were discussing the CCR amongst themselves. I started to get loads of feedback — disproportionately negative.

Several of the elder statesmen of the firm, brokers who had been around for decades, would call me after each edition of the newsletter to point out flaws in my logic. I had reached out to these same men when I first started working at the firm to learn from their expertise, as an apprentice of sorts, and they wouldn't give me the time of day. Now they were unloading decades worth of experiential wisdom on me every time they disagreed with my analysis.

It may not have been their intention, but they were providing me with a valuable education. They always felt that I was undervaluing one data point or another, especially when my forecast contradicted their existing positions. In most cases they were right, or at least had a valid point, which drove me to greater lengths to ensure that my research and analysis was airtight. I spent evenings studying markets that I was not yet trading in, like sugar and coffee, for the purpose of improving my forecasts. It was an amazing learning experience, and an unintended benefit of publishing the newsletter.

It would not be long before my extracurricular research into these markets yielded a profit.

CHAPTER 14

ICED COFFEE

When I first began trading commodities, I relied almost entirely on technical analysis because that was all I knew. It was not within my skillset to beat the market at fundamental analysis like predicting changes in industrial demand or silver mine output, much less decisions by the Federal Reserve or Treasury Department.

As I expanded my knowledge and experience over the years, I relied more and more on fundamental factors, but I never lost my ability to spot a strong technical indicator when it presented itself.

While studying a chart of coffee prices in 1994, I recognized a familiar formation. This was before everyone had trading software with algorithms to identify such patterns. The trend lines had to be drawn with a pencil on graph paper.

Fortunately, I didn't need fancy software to tell me that I was looking at a classic bull flag. The fundamentals also looked strong, as far as I could tell, and there was potential help on the way from harsh weather. All of this supported a bullish stance, so I advised my clients to go long.

There were not many coffee traders in the Midwest at the time, certainly not in Milwaukee, so people noticed when I started buying a significant quantity of futures. The trading community was small, and people talked. Anytime someone deviated from convention, colleagues would either criticize or copy them.

When I bought coffee for around $0.80 per pound it caused local industry gossip. When freezing temperatures in Brazil's coffee-growing region caused the price to surpass $2.00 a pound, it became headline news in the business section.

I received a phone call from Michael Fritz, a journalist for *Crain's Chicago Business*, requesting to schedule an interview about the coffee market. I was excited to be featured prominently in a highly respected publication. He and I spent nearly an hour on the phone discussing all the reasons I had been so bullish on coffee, and what I expected to happen next. I was pleased with my performance during the conversation, as I managed to avoid patting myself on the back too hard. I expected to come across very well in the article.

Toward the end of the interview, seemingly as a throwaway question, Fritz asked if any of my investors would be willing to speak with him. I gave him the phone number of a favorite client of mine named Ladd, a good ol' boy from Alabama who always had plenty to say. Ladd netted over half a million dollars on that coffee trade, so I knew that after initially giving Fritz an earful he would have glowing things to say about me.

The issue of *Crain's* came out on July 16, and I bought one on my way into the office. I immediately spotted the article I was looking for: "Jolting the Java Market" by Michael Fritz.

I scanned it looking for my name, but I wasn't mentioned. Ladd was quoted as saying, "This kind of opportunity only comes around once in a decade." Apparently, they were not interested in my detailed analysis, but instead needed something simple and concise. Lesson learned.

The coffee trade raised my profile within Allendale. I was one of the few brokers trading soft commodities, and my clients had just made a killing. We rolled the profits into sugar, which I wrote about in the next edition of the *Cordier Commodity Report*.

Late one afternoon, a few weeks later, my phone rang again. It was a colleague from headquarters whom I had never met. He only knew my name because of CCR. He said, "There's a reporter on the line who wants to speak with you." With no further explanation, the call was patched through.

"Hello Mr. Cordier, this is Chris Thompson from Reuters. I understand you're the resident sugar expert. Would you be willing to answer a few questions?"

CHAPTER 15

THE SUGAR BEAT

G rowth of global sugar consumption, which had held steady at about 2% annually for decades, was slowing. This was due, in part, to economic conditions in the former Soviet Union. The Evil Empire had collapsed just a few years prior, and the former communist nations were in disarray. Their citizens did not have the disposable income necessary for luxury food items, and the infrastructure to import them no longer existed. At first glance this would have been a bearish indicator, but deeper analysis revealed a contradictory fact pattern.

Most farmland can grow a variety of crops. A vital component of agribusiness is forecasting where prices will be months or years in advance, to choose which type of seeds to plant. Farmers develop a granular understanding of the markets for their products, and often anticipate softening in demand long before so-called market prognosticators.

As a result, many sugar growers in 1994 had preemptively shifted acreage to what they expected to be more profitable crops. After the seeds were in the ground, unexpected flooding negatively affected the sugar-beet-producing regions of the United States, further diminishing the size of the global sugar harvest. Additionally, while speculators paid close attention to how the collapse of the USSR would hurt demand for sugar, many failed to see how it would impact supply.

Cuba had been the world's leading producer of sugar cane back when it was supported by the Soviet Union. Since the collapse, however, Cuba experienced a 40% decline in yield due to shortages of fertilizer, pesticides, fuel, and equipment.

Factoring all that information together, I expected global sugar consumption to exceed production by over one million tons, dropping stockpiles to a four-year low and driving up the price.

I wish I had the presence of mind to mention all of that to the reporter.

But instead, with no time to prepare for the unexpected call, I managed to utter simply, "The fundamentals are bullish, the technicals are bullish — sugar is good."

Not the most eloquent statement, but brief and decisive enough to be quoted in the article, which was picked up by the *New York Times*.

After that quote appeared in the business section of several large newspapers, I expected to receive at least a couple of calls from prospective clients who had read my prophetic words. No calls came. I realized that I would need to be more prepared for the next phone call from the media. I would have to be concise and decisive, but also say something meaningful.

I worked at condensing my analysis into a useful sound bite that had substance. The media may have been the motivation for this effort, but it proved most helpful when discussing strategic concepts with investors. Some clients are completely hands-off, while others like to know the thought process behind each trade.

Six months later, after sugar rallied, the same reporter called again. I hoped that he was working on a follow-up article about my stellar forecast. It turned out that he didn't necessarily remember writing that article, but he had made a note next to my name indicating that I was willing to give an unvarnished opinion on the market.

Professional wealth managers are hesitant to give strong predictions to the media, presumably because they do not wish to be wrong publicly. They always include caveats, hedges, ifs, buts, and maybes. All of these qualifiers are valid and should be included in a long form article or research report, but they obfuscate the message when space is limited. The press was always looking for a concise statement, so they loved "sugar is good." I was on their speed dial now.

Chris Thompson and I developed a great working relationship and friendship. He occasionally called me for comments, or just to help him with research. On my next trip to New York, he showed me around the Reuters offices and brought me to lunch at Smith & Wollensky (which became a ritual every time I visited the Big Apple). I also made my first visit to the World Trade Center to meet with silver traders whom I had previously only dealt with on the phone. I found they were much more frank during in-person conversations, especially during happy hour, and had plenty of useful insights. I learned a great deal about their side of the business. They introduced me to decision makers in other markets that I was interested in pursuing.

Though I had been heralded as an authority on the sugar market, in truth it accounted for just a tiny percentage of my portfolio. Allendale had given me some latitude to trade as I wished, but it wasn't complete freedom. Despite my success in coffee, it preferred I stay predominantly within the domain of Chicago commodities. That meant grains and livestock. Precious metals and energy were okay because those markets are ubiquitous, but sugar, cotton, cocoa, and coffee were viewed as New York commodities. I traded mostly small quantities in these markets, testing my hypotheses.

During subsequent trips to New York, I met with some of the biggest traders in the soft commodity markets. We exchanged ideas and strategies, and it was clear that I was ready to trade in the big leagues.

CHAPTER 16

LOW-HANGING FRUIT

A s a kid in Wisconsin, I had different part-time jobs for different times of the year. The employment and transportation options were somewhat limited for a 12-year-old, so I had to make the most of what was available. My father taught me to appreciate the sore muscles obtained from hours spent mowing lawns, raking leaves, or shoveling snow. The pain and fatigue served as confirmation I had done an honest day's work.

My favorite job was picking cherries, one of the two things Door County is most famous for (the other being shipbuilding). The cherry harvest came around every summer for just a few weeks and I had it circled on my calendar well in advance.

Anyone could show up to pick cherries, and the orchard would pay 50 cents per pail. It was mostly a recreational activity for tourists from Milwaukee or Chicago who drove up for the weekend. They would choose one tree and casually pick fruit from the lower branches, maybe get a ladder and pick a few from the middle branches, but they would give up long before reaching the top of the tree. What little money they earned was usually spent in the gift shop before they left.

By the end of a typical Saturday afternoon, the trees were left barren at the bottom but still had plenty of ripe cherries on top. I was determined to devise an efficient method of collecting the remaining fruit from those upper limbs. I stayed late into the afternoon and early evening, long after the crowds had left, trying various methods — recklessly stretching from the top rung of the ladder, climbing the tree, shaking the trunk, even throwing a football at the top branches and trying to catch the cherries that got knocked loose. Each attempt was either dangerous, ineffective, or both. At the end of the day I was bruised, splintered, blistered, and exhausted. What did I get out of all that effort? Not much.

The solution had been literally right in front of my face. Rather than obsess over the hard-to-reach cherries, the best methodology was to ignore the top and even the middle branches, and just go for the lower limbs. The low-hanging fruit yielded the greatest return with the lowest cost (in terms of energy expenditure) and lowest risk (of injury).

At first, this seemed contradictory to what I had learned from my father about hard work. It's not that he was wrong, but there is some nuance to this value. Work hard but be strategic about where to focus your efforts.

After getting permission from the orchard manager, I devised an efficient plan. I arrived at the orchard shortly after dawn, long before the first tourists, and focused exclusively on the low branches. I hustled from tree to tree, filling multiple pails with lightning speed. In about two hours I picked more cherries than I used to get in an entire day. I was still exhausted, splintered, and stained with red juice. However, I had made twice the money in half the time while eliminating the risk of breaking my neck.

Cherry season was highly profitable that year, enabling me to add significantly to my silver collection. However, the following summer the orchard implemented a rule against "creaming the crop," which was their name for my low-hanging fruit strategy. It had been good while it lasted.

Cherry season was brief, and my jobs during the other 50 weeks of the year were intermittent and largely dependent on the weather. When my older brother Patrick turned 16, he obtained a driver's license, which allowed him to take a job across town stocking shelves at Super Value, the local grocery store.

Patrick was now consistently working upwards of 20 hours per week. This had a compounding effect on his savings, not only because he was being paid more, but also because he had less free time in which to spend his hard-earned money. Soon he was flush with cash, and I had an idea that would help both of us.

For years I had been allocating nearly every penny I earned toward buying silver, but it wasn't enough. I started an entity called Jim's Coin Company and offered Patrick an opportunity to invest. We came to an unusual agreement whereby he would contribute a portion of his grocery store salary, in perpetuity, in exchange for a 2% stake in my coin company. The whole family joked about how I was a miser for offering such a small percentage, but I was convinced that this enterprise would become the largest coin merchant in Wisconsin. Heck, maybe even the whole Midwest!

The deal fell apart within months, after Patrick got a girlfriend. He decided that spending his salary taking her out on the town was more important than owning a preposterously small stake in his kid brother's company, so he asked me to buy him out. Decades later, our family teased Patrick that he would've done well to hold onto that 2%.

CHAPTER 17

COFFEE CALLS

I was still trying to raise capital without resorting to the high-pressure sales tactics that I had witnessed at other firms. Being quoted in the media was nice, but it was not bringing clients to my doorstep. I discovered that the most effective way to ethically increase my assets under management was to give my existing clients something to talk about. The coffee trade had done that to some extent. Clients boasted about it with their friends, and that led to a few referrals.

My clients were sophisticated investors and had a multitude of wealth managers guiding them in the stock market, real estate, and other ventures. They understood that true diversification has tremendous value. Commodities were a small slice of their overall investment portfolio.

I tried to differentiate myself from my peers by providing unique insights and recommendations. That meant further diversifying within the commodity domain. My clients already had financial advisors telling them to buy gold, and everyone had an opinion on the price of oil, but how many of them were making money in sugar, cotton, or coffee? Not many.

To take risk outside the normal pantheon of investments, they needed a reason. If I failed to demonstrate the rationale behind the strategy and the uniqueness of what I offered, the actual returns were merely a number on a spreadsheet at the end of the year. The more I explained the logic behind my decisions, the more they wanted to invest.

Coffee futures react sharply to weather reports during the Southern Hemisphere's winter, and every year they seemed to rally on drought concerns until the spring's first rain appeared. Brazil is by far the dominant producer of Arabica, which is generally considered the higher quality variety of the coffee plant. Indonesia and Vietnam produce Robusta, which becomes an attractive substitute when the price of Arabica rises too high. If the price of both varieties goes high enough, consumers may switch to tea or other caffeinated beverages. There are many causes for short-term volatility in coffee, but also many equalizing factors that balance supply and demand in the long run.

Speculators viewed coffee as being price inelastic because consumers are unwilling to part with their morning cup of joe. This is true up to a certain point, but at the end of the day coffee is not truly a necessity. This means the price elasticity is not smooth, it's sticky. Demand remains relatively constant as a function of price, until it reaches a tipping point and begins to fall sharply.

Much of my analysis was based on research and reporting conducted by Judith Ganes, a soft commodity analyst at Merrill Lynch. She seemed to be the most informed person about the coffee market. I asked my reporter friend, Chris Thompson, if he could put me in touch with her.

"I don't know her. Have you tried calling her?" Chris asked.

In my mind, the mind of a fledgling coffee trader, Judith Ganes was a big celebrity. I didn't think it was possible to just call her out of the blue. I asked Chris if he knew where I might be able to find her number, assuming the press had a classified database of high-profile people.

"Yes," Chris replied, in a matter-of-fact tone but not sure whether my question had been a joke, "It's called the phone book."

It was obvious but had not occurred to me. I called Merrill's headquarters and asked to speak with her. It took a few transfers, and leaving a message with her assistant, but within a week we were on the phone discussing soft markets. I was still green as a coffee trader and appreciated the chance to learn from an expert. I think she was just happy to have a fellow coffee nerd to talk shop with.

Judith and I spoke several more times over the course of the next couple of years. I tried to come up with unorthodox ideas, things she hadn't already considered. In that pursuit, I looked closely at what was happening on the coffee plantations in Brazil and discovered a major change that had been overlooked by many traders.

During the first half of 1997, the price of coffee spiked well above $2.00 per pound once again due to cold temperatures in the Southern Hemisphere. This led coffee traders in early 1998, having experienced extreme rallies twice in the previous four years, to be on the lookout for bad weather. As rain failed to show up and potential cold fronts did, the price began to rise modestly. Short-sellers in that market, still licking their wounds from the previous year, were hesitant to sell.

On the surface it looked like another strong buying opportunity. My clients fondly remembered the previous year's coffee rally and were eager to ring that bell again. They called daily to ask why we hadn't bought any coffee yet. The weather patterns in Southern Brazil were similar, but the plantations had moved. After the frost of 1994, coffee growers began migrating north to warmer regions. And by 1998, those new trees were bearing fruit.

A wonderful thing about investing in commodities is that almost all the pertinent information is publicly available if you're willing to dig. It's like having inside information for trading a stock, except it's perfectly legitimate.

Knowing that Brazilian farmers had moved their coffee trees to warmer plantations was a tremendous advantage. It was not exactly a secret, but farmers had an incentive not to advertise the fact that another frost-damaged crop was unlikely.

Though I believed coffee futures were slightly overpriced at the beginning of 1998, I was unwilling to sell them. It seemed likely that coffee would become more overpriced before the eventual collapse, and trying to pick the exact top or bottom of a volatile market is a fool's errand.

The inherent drawback of using leverage to speculate in the futures market is the precision with which you must trade. If you buy futures, and the price pulls back 5% before going up 10%, it's likely you would have been shaken out of the position before the rally took place. The forecast can ultimately be accurate, but the trade still loses money.

I noticed there was high demand for "lottery tickets" in coffee, meaning speculators were buying far out-of-the-money call options with strike prices in excess of $3.00 per pound. Opportunistic bulls were hedging their long futures positions by selling those calls, which were trading at unreasonably high premiums. There was only *one* leg of that trade that looked attractive to me.

I believe that commodities are generally priced at their fair value most of the time, which is why I rarely take an extremely bullish or bearish stance. The efficient market theory works in aggregate, but inefficiencies exist within it and can be exploited. Often, these opportunities come in the form of mispriced options. The underlying commodity may be priced fairly, but the risk sometimes is not.

On a day-to-day basis, commodity trading is rooted in under-standing seasonality and trends, and how a commodity typically responds to specific market influences. It's about consistently playing the percentages and getting base hits, not swinging for the fences. Many successful commodity investors make the same trades every year, with only slight adjustments.

On rare occasions though, the stars line up for a big one-off opportunity. In 1994 and 1997, the big opportunity in coffee was the result of a frost threatening to destroy the harvest. In 1998, the big opportunity came from a false belief that it might happen again.

By strategically selling options, it was possible to make money predicting what *wasn't* going to happen. This seemed like a smarter way of investing.

CHAPTER 18

ALUMINUM AND IVORY

B y 1999, the internet had made it possible to trade and access information from virtually anywhere, so there was no longer a competitive advantage to living in the proximity of Midwest farms and Chicago trading pits.

Sensing I had outgrown my Milwaukee office, Allendale offered me the opportunity to relocate anywhere in the country. I knew I would miss being a few hours' drive from my family in Sturgeon Bay, so I spent a good deal of time up there while I pondered the decision of where I wanted to live for the rest of my life.

By this time, Patrick had taken a job at the Palmer Johnsons shipyard in town. Because I had always been enamored with boats, he gave me a tour of the cavernous dry-dock where he worked. The shipyard was completing a 193-foot aluminum yacht for the king of Spain. As we stood there looking at the impressive ship, a crane lifted a Steinway grand piano and swung it high above our heads toward the main deck.

Patrick remarked, *"Who in the hell needs a piano on a boat?"*

I suppose nobody needs a piano on a boat, but I thought it was cool. The yachts, cargo ships, and Navy vessels that came through our town were evidence that there was a big, exciting world out there. There were great fortunes waiting to be made. Why shouldn't someone put a piano on a boat if they can afford it?

I realized it was time to relocate. My lifelong passion for boating meant I should live in a place where I could enjoy being on the water for more than just a few months a year. I had been monitoring weather patterns in Florida for nearly two decades and had no doubt that it would be a great place to set up shop. Reading reports of winter temperatures around 70 degrees Fahrenheit, whilst freezing my tail off in Wisconsin, made it easy to see the upside. The absence of a state income tax played a role as well.

Miami was the obvious choice due to its beaches, culture, restaurants, nightlife, and international airport. It also just happens to be a major hub for the international coffee trade. But I didn't want to just go with the obvious choice, so I did more research.

I knew from studying orange crops that the Gulf Coast was far less likely to be directly impacted by a hurricane. Tropical storms travel from the southeast to the northwest on their way to the Gulf of Mexico, meaning that any storm reaching the west coast of the state is likely to have already travelled across the peninsula, causing it to weaken substantially.

The Tampa Bay region boasts some of the most beautiful beaches in the world, great restaurants, excellent sports teams, and near perfect weather nine months of the year. Many current and potential clients owned homes in the surrounding cities of Tampa, St. Petersburg, Clearwater, and Sarasota. It was still a small metropolis in 1999, but with the baby-boom generation set to begin retiring soon, the region was certain to grow. I decided to move there, and it has been my primary home ever since.

CHAPTER 19

SUNSHINE STATE OF MIND

T he relocation to Florida was revitalizing, but professionally I was still feeling constrained. Allendale had generally been a great company to work for, but it was no longer a good fit for the type of trading I wanted to pursue, namely selling overpriced options on commodity futures.

To serve my clients to the best of my ability, I needed full decision-making authority over their portfolios. After nearly a decade with Allendale, we parted ways amicably. It had been a great experience working with the owner, Paul Georgy. I learned a great deal, and I'm still grateful for my time there. I explored a few other firms but ultimately decided to open my own brokerage, which I later converted to a Commodity Trading Advisor or CTA (A CTA is an individual or firm that provides trading advice on futures and options. In many cases, the CTA has discretionary authority to manage the client's account, which must first be opened with a Futures Clearing Merchant (FCM)).

By outsourcing the back-office operations and custodianship of the funds, a CTA is more streamlined than a major institutional brokerage house. I would no longer have access to a large research department, but by that point most of the data I needed was available on the internet.

The risk/reward of starting the new enterprise was uncertain in financial terms, but money was not the only motivating factor. The thing that ultimately swayed me was the freedom to operate as I saw fit. With that sentiment in mind, I named my firm Liberty Trading Group and opened an office in St. Petersburg, Florida.

Not long after setting up the new company, our receptionist, Farah, received a phone call from another commodity broker who was right across the bay, in Tampa. He mentioned that he had been reading the *Wall Street Journal* and noticed my name quoted in the commodity section that day. He asked if he could come by the office and introduce himself. I thought, "What, another commodities broker here on the west coast of Florida? And he reads the *Journal*?"

I told Farah to set up a meeting. The broker was Michael Gross, a bright ambitious young man who was also originally from the Midwest. He arrived in a well-tailored dark suit, a relatively rare sight in St. Pete at the time. He shared his background and passion for the business with me. He struck me as an individual with genuine interest in the world of commodities. We chatted for an hour or two, and at the end we shook hands and brought up the idea of meeting again soon.

When visiting Chicago, you will hear people talking about corn and soybeans during happy hour at any tavern in The Loop. Visiting New York, it would be conversations of gold, silver, and the price of crude that day at Smith & Wollensky's. Tampa has transformed over the last two decades into a vibrant and well-established business community, but at the time I relocated there in 1999 it was far from that. Having the chance to discuss markets with someone like Michael was refreshing.

We had a few more conversations over the ensuing weeks and discovered that we were on the same page when it came to market analysis and trading strategy. Michael's style of client engagement was somewhat different from mine in that he was proactive, whereas I tended to focus solely on trading and let the customer acquisition occur organically. I did little marketing aside from my quarterly newsletter and the occasional media appearance. I did no prospecting whatsoever. Michael helped me realize just how much potential I was leaving on the table.

Initially I had no plans to expand the size of my company, but it quickly became evident that Michael's skillset complimented my own greatly. I offered him a position with Liberty Trading and was elated when he accepted. I knew that with the two of us working together, we had an opportunity to build something special.

CHAPTER 20

DARK CLOUDS

M ichael brilliantly handled aspects of the business that I had been neglecting, primarily marketing. He took ideas from our strategy meetings and typed them into articles that were distributed through multiple platforms. He corresponded with prospective clients for months, in some cases years, before they were ready to open an account. He was very much in tune with my long-held philosophy of being an open book. Let people know what we trade, and why. The difference was that now the message was reaching a much wider audience.

The feedback from investors was overwhelmingly positive, as they appreciated receiving answers to all their questions without any pressure to commit. If they wanted to invest, great. If not, that was okay too. Michael was taking a long-term approach to building our client relationships, just as I was taking a long-term approach toward trading.

Markets were impacted by several unprecedented events during Liberty Trading's first few years. The growth of technology companies was starting to look like a bubble, which persuaded savvy investors to take a portion of their wealth out of the stock market and diversify into commodities. Though we laugh about it now, the Y2K panic injected serious implied volatility into option markets at the time. As did the chaos surrounding the 2000 U.S. Presidential Election.

These issues paled in comparison to what Americans would experience next.

When the September 11th attacks occurred, my first thought was concern for the traders I had met over the years, as well as the thousands of other innocent victims who worked in the World Trade Center. I watched it unfold on television, along with the rest of America. I thought, *I've been in those buildings. This can't be happening. Such a devastating tragedy, unlike anything we've ever seen.*

My second thought was about the hundreds of millions of dollars in bullion stored in the basement of the buildings. There was a reported 379,000 ounces of gold and nearly 30 million ounces of silver in those vaults. Everyone knew it was there, beneath half a million tons of rubble. Would they dig it out? Could they dig it out? Did it melt? How will this affect the price of precious metals?

My third thought was about how the United States would respond to the attack, and the fallout that it would have on all commodity prices. The impact of major events like this on the market is sometimes the opposite of what one would expect.

People assume that the price of gold must have spiked tremendously that day. Actually, there was a rally of 6% on the European exchanges, which seemed mild considering the gravity of the event. When the New York exchanges reopened a few days later, investors began selling their positions in gold, presumably to cover their margin calls in the stock market and other investments that fell due to the terrorist attack.

By November 24, the price of gold had fallen all the way back below $272 per ounce, its opening price on 9/11. But the chain of events and government spending that had been set off that day needed time to develop. Shock-and-awe now, inflation later. Within five years the price of gold would reach $600. Within 10 years, it surpassed $1,800.

Michael experienced a real baptism by fire in his first couple of years working with me at Liberty. From the tech bubble to Y2K, to 9/11 and the wars that followed. Those were difficult years to be a trader, especially one that specialized in selling volatility. But we were able to remain one step ahead of the market. For the most part.

CHAPTER 21

RUNNING OF THE BULLS

War in the Middle East was weighing heavily on energy markets, creating both opportunities and risk. The price of oil has tremendous downstream effects on other commodities, so rather than speculate on it directly we diversified strategically.

Higher fuel prices increase the cost of farming which leads to higher grain prices, which in turn leads to higher cost of production of cattle and hogs. There were other reasons to be bullish on livestock, as the popular Atkins diet had people eating more beef and pork.

As our agricultural system became more mechanized and commodified, it was forced to rely more heavily on fertilizer, pesticides, antibiotics, and massive livestock feedlots. This may be necessary to feed seven billion people, but, as with every technological advancement, it has unintended consequences. When something goes wrong in a large complex system, it tends to go wrong on a massive scale.

Traders generally regard the last week or two of the year as a quiet time in the markets. Decision makers tend to save any big moves until after the new year, and many traders go on vacation. Trading volume is generally thin, which hurts liquidity. This is truer of equity markets than it is of commodities because agriculture is more heavily impacted by natural (nonhuman) forces. Weather events and outbreaks of disease in crops or livestock do not wait until after the holidays.

The Christmas season is a reminder of the orange juice rally in 1983, and how having fewer traders at their desks likely exacerbated the problem. That's why I always remained vigilant through the end of the year. That being said, I tried to dip out for two days before Christmas to visit my family in Sturgeon Bay, feeling safe knowing that Michael was at the helm. I would be in front of my laptop during market hours regardless.

I was in line at the airport when my phone rang. It was Chris Thompson from Reuters.

"Are you in front of your computer?"

"No, I'm in line at the airport," which was still figuring out its post-9/11 security protocols, causing unbearable wait times.

"It's all over the television, too."

"What is?"

"Mad Cow."

I dropped the phone.

The first case of Bovine Spongiform Encephalopathy, otherwise known as "mad cow disease," had been reported in the United States.

After picking up my phone and getting through security, I called Michael who was at home wrapping Christmas gifts. He answered after half of a ring.

"I just saw it on the news," he said. "I'm looking at the strikes we have on now, trying to come up with the best gameplan."

We had about 25% of our portfolio tied up in short cattle puts, a position that was about to lose a lot of money.

The images on the television news in the airport lounge were jarring, showing cattle stumbling around and falling over. It was a sad sight to see for everyone, but especially me. It was after market hours, but cattle futures were going to get slaughtered the moment trading resumed the next day.

Sure enough, the next morning live cattle went limit down and futures trading was halted. Options continued to trade even when the underlying futures contract was locked, meaning that we had the ability to buy back our short positions on the open market. This is one of the advantages of trading options, however just because we had the ability to buy them didn't mean it was a good idea.

Cattle futures traders, unable to close out of their long futures positions, raced to buy options in desperation, driving up premiums. Those were the same options that we were short.

Because we had diversified into several commodity classes, and kept a significant cash reserve, we were not forced to close out of our position in cattle. Once the initial panic had passed, and market-wide margin calls were dealt with, volatility would come back to rational levels. Our portfolio strategy gave us the freedom to wait a few days and get out at a much better price. We survived the Black Angus black swan.

CHAPTER 22

COMPLETE GUIDE TO OPTION SELLING

Commodity futures and options have a language all their own, which can be confusing even to professional investors if they are inexperienced in these markets. After decades in the industry, traders get accustomed to using jargon that most people do not understand, making the subject matter sound more complicated than it is. I believe this is why many investors are intimidated by commodities and derivatives.

Michael had a natural gift for explaining complex topics in terms that our clients could understand. They were all intelligent and experienced investors, so the key was to simplify the verbiage but not the concepts.

In 2003 we were contacted by McGraw Hill about writing a book on option trading. There was a growing interest in the subject, but professional traders were hesitant to share their secrets with the public. The library contained textbooks on theoretical option mathematics written by university professors, as well as colorful trading manuals with titles like *Options for Imbeciles*. The publisher was interested in a useful guide for smart investors who wanted to learn about selling options, written by somebody who did it every day.

I was excited by the prospect, but apprehensive due to the time it would require. Michael was adamant that we could do it. The most time-consuming aspect of writing such a book is the research that goes into it, but we were already conducting the research as portfolio managers. All we would have to do was translate or explain some of the industry jargon. There would be no agenda to the book, it did not have to be polished, it would simply describe our market philosophy and experiences.

There was risk in peeling the curtain back too far. Perhaps other CTAs would start making the same trades as us, reducing liquidity and profitability. Perhaps some of our clients, after reading the book, would decide they could manage their own portfolio and didn't need us anymore.

Ultimately, we had faith that the market was big enough to accommodate a few more traders, and there were plenty of investors who had neither the time nor inclination to do the amount of research necessary to manage a diversified portfolio. We weren't sure it was going to work, but we went for it. For about the next year, Michael and I spent our days on research and trading and our evenings and weekends writing the book.

The Complete Guide to Option Selling was essentially a textbook about commodity options. Unlike other textbooks, there was no college course requiring students to buy it, so we did not expect sales to flourish as they did. It had a tremendous impact on our business, in both intended and unintended ways.

Liberty Trading started to receive emails and phone calls from readers. Some wanted to open an account, while others were seeking additional details or clarifications of topics they had read about. Farah took notes on the feedback for us. As first-time authors, Michael and I knew there would be room for improvement.

Our publisher arranged several press interviews in New York City to coincide with the book release, and things snowballed from there. The interviews with CNBC and Bloomberg Television went well, and they invited me back. Media appearances fueled book sales, and the book sales fueled more interest from the media.

After the book promotion ended, I continued making guest appearances on the financial news cable networks. This was before Zoom, when interviews were conducted "live, via satellite." I routinely drove across the bay to the NBC affiliate station in Tampa where I sat in front of a camera while an anchor in New York City asked questions pertaining to commodity markets.

The networks called me whenever a commodity story broke, temporarily shifting their focus away from the stock market. Often it was a geopolitical situation causing a rise in gasoline prices, or a looming hurricane threatening Florida's orange groves.

Those were the topics viewers tuned in for, they were not as interested in hearing me discuss the latest WASDE report. That was an adjustment for me because I don't often tell people what they want to hear. I tell them the truth or my honest opinion, or I say nothing at all.

The press is always seeking a bold proclamation that will generate a buzz, especially on television where it can be hotly debated with other experts. I was happy to provide such a statement when it was sincere, but my analysis often found that the topic we were discussing either had already been baked into the price for weeks or would have minimal impact.

My answers didn't necessarily make for sensational television, but they were sincere. There are ways to make money in a stagnant market, and I believed that was a worthwhile discussion for the audience to hear. Options, and specifically option-selling, were of tremendous interest to investors.

CHAPTER 23

ETHANOL-BASED CORN

The United States is the largest producer of corn in the world. The climate and soil in North America make it relatively cheap and easy to grow. For the average American, the mention of corn evokes the image of an ear full of plump yellow kernels slathered in butter, or a bucket of movie theater popcorn, but those types of corn account for less than one percent of total production.

Ninety-nine percent of corn acreage in the United States is dedicated to field corn, which you wouldn't want to sink your teeth into in its natural state. Its primary use is for livestock feed, and it can be industrially processed into foods for human consumption, like cereal and high-fructose corn syrup. In the early 2000s, as the price of crude oil rose, another use of field corn emerged from relative obscurity to consuming one-third of all the corn grown in the USA.

Ethanol is an alcohol, typically made from fermented plants, which can be used effectively as a replacement for gasoline. It is the primary automotive fuel source in Brazil, where it is derived from sugarcane, which grows abundantly there and is easily refined.

Corn-based ethanol is less efficient to produce. It is not an economically viable choice to take the place of gasoline, but Americans had grown wary of depending on an increasingly unstable Middle East for their energy needs.

A large swath of the electoral map has a corn-based economy. Iowa, the nation's top producer of corn, just so happens to be the first state to cast ballots in the presidential primary season every four years. These facts have led to government subsidies and mandates to help this industry, and ethanol was the newest iteration of that. Commodity speculators paid close attention, and hedge funds spent fortunes building their corn-trading operations.

Open-outcry trading had been in decline for years, as electronic order execution began to account for an increasingly significant share of volume. By 2005, The New York Stock Exchange's trading floor was little more than a charade for television cameras.

Futures markets, like the Chicago Mercantile Exchange, were slower to make the transition to full electronic trading because the old system still had value. The complexity of derivative contracts meant there was still a need for open-outcry trading floors.

Instead of a simple binary bid/ask price, speculators and bona-fide hedgers rely heavily on knowing the depth and size of the market. Additionally, many commodity market participants require price quotations for complex option spreads, which can choose from dozens of expiration dates and hundreds of strike prices in a potentially infinite number of combinations.

This nuance still required a human element because artificial intelligence was not yet up to the task. Even so, most of the trading floors at the commodity exchanges were noticeably less crowded than they had been in prior decades. One exception was the corn pit, which experienced a renaissance after Congress enacted an ethanol mandate in 2005.

In 2003, the entire grain room at the Chicago Board of Trade had been populated by a few dozen old-timers with paper price charts in the pockets of their trading vests. However, by 2006, ethanol had revitalized the trading floor. The corn pit alone was packed and surrounded with over a hundred hedge-fund wunderkinds. They were pressed together like sardines, tapping away on tablet computers. The computers were connected to their home offices, which were constantly updating proprietary algorithms. They were able to instantly generate prices for complicated derivatives based on innumerable data points.

Market-makers, taking cues from their tablets, screamed and shouted and got in fights as they competed over trades. It was reminiscent of my first visit to the trading floor in the early 1980s. An interesting melding of the old ways with new technology.

The fervor of the corn traders had me wondering if I was missing something. Clearly there was no chance of ethanol overtaking gasoline as our primary fuel, but people were buying futures and call options as if that was going to happen. This looked like a bubble that could continue for some time but was ultimately unsustainable.

The sensational claims about ethanol never came true. It remains as an additive in our gasoline, but it never took over as a legitimate energy source without subsidies and mandates. This eventual outcome had been evident from the beginning. Strategically selling far-out-of-the-money options during this period proved to be a winning strategy.

CHAPTER 24

PEAK OIL

The city of Tampa had been growing steadily since I moved there, beginning a transition from sleepy destination for retirees to a legitimate economic center. While it was not New York or Chicago, Tampa was on its way. I wanted to be in the middle of that growth, so in 2007 I moved my primary office across the bay, from St. Pete to downtown Tampa, where it has been ever since. The bigger city facilitated meetings with local business leaders, allowed me to quickly drop into the television station for midday interviews, and provided easy access to the international airport.

In the spring of 2008, I went to New York to meet with media outlets in preparation for the launch of the second edition of the book. It had become a custom to meet colleagues at Smith

& Wollensky whenever I was in town. Normally, the place was packed with investment industry professionals and the conversations at the bar were lively. On this occasion, however, the mood at S&W was very different. The restaurant was empty.

I asked the bartender where everyone was, and he pointed at the television which was tuned into one of the financial news networks. The anchors looked as if they'd seen a ghost, and the headline banner said something about the Bear Stearns collapse. I was aware that this had taken place but hadn't personally related to the gravity of the event until that moment. The firm's offices were in the same neighborhood as the restaurant, and the feeling in the air was heavy. A financial crash is like a car crash; in the immediate aftermath victims struggle to comprehend what just happened. Businessmen in $5,000 suits wandered the sidewalks aimlessly in disbelief.

When the financial crisis of 2007-2008 hit, the tangible nature of physical commodities provided a certain degree of stability as compared to stocks and bonds, but volatility permeates throughout securities markets. Investors will sell their best-performing assets to cover the margin call from their stock portfolio. Additionally, the uncertainty regarding the strength of the global economy, as well as the future of interest rates and inflation, caused volatility in commodity prices.

A global economic slowdown would put some commodities at greater risk of softening demand than others. With the origins of the Great Recession being in the housing market, building materials like lumber and copper faced the most peril. Discretionary items like cotton, coffee, and cocoa were in some danger. Energy tends to be resilient, but tightening pocketbooks would lead consumers to travel less and moderate their thermostats at home. Grains and livestock would be fine, as long as Americans continued to eat. Precious metals are a category unto themselves, as the "flight to quality" does not always go as expected.

In many ways, the so-called Great Recession was business as usual for us. The disruption to commodity markets was of the type we anticipate seeing every few years. It was not a once-in-a-generation crash as it was for the banking industry, but option prices remained inflated across the board.

By the summer of 2008, Liberty Trading was running like a well-oiled machine, and all eyes in the commodity world were on the price of crude. Oil prices had been relentlessly climbing higher due to increased demand from developing nations, environmentalist push-back on drilling, and wars in the Middle East, which were beginning to look like they'd never end. Americans had by now come to the realization that corn-based ethanol was not the solution to our energy woes.

Many a talking head had come on television during the previous 12 months to say that oil would never top $100 per barrel, then it would never reach $120, then $130.

All were proven wrong, and the goalposts kept moving until they were dismantled completely. Eventually, many of those same analysts completely reversed course and there was a media chorus singing about the potential for $150 oil, or even $200.

I was receiving more media requests than I knew what to do with, so I would pick and choose. Fox Business Network was an upstart at that time, creating some much-needed competition in market news, and Neil Cavuto is a solid professional, so I was happy to appear on his program.

Neil had me on for a "Best in Class" segment that featured analysts who had been consistently accurate in the past. Often, during these types of appearances, the market move I was there to discuss had already been pushed beyond its fair value by trend-following speculators. Professional analysts always seem to be bearish at the bottom and bullish at the top.

Bearish crude oil traders had been run-over, stopped-out, and margin-called several times by this point. After such a prolonged rally, few were willing or able to stick their neck out by taking a short position. They were hyper focused on what oil had done over the previous year, preventing them from clearly evaluating the present circumstances. The fundamental drivers of the crude oil rally had stalled, and momentum was the only thing keeping it going. The normal rules of supply and demand had become disjointed, and that is where option-selling opportunities lie.

One of the most basic truisms of commodity trading is that high prices cure high prices. When a product becomes too expensive, consumers buy less of it, causing the price to fall. A misapplication of this credo is what led the previous short-sellers of oil to their demise. They were certain that as the price of crude continued to climb, eventually it would reach a point where consumption would drop, thus ending the rally. The primary factors they overlooked were taking place in China.

China was the elephant in the room, and had been for some time, so economists and market analysts were constantly crunching their numbers. They analyzed every numerical data point to project how much China's GDP would grow over the next year, or several years. The factor that was being overlooked by the quants was more qualitative than quantitative, as is usually the case when paradigms change.

Although China was an economic powerhouse, if you had visited any of its cities in the year 2000 you would have noticed a lot more bicycles and rickshaws than automobiles. Cars were only for the rich. As GDP rose over the years, auto sales grew at a glacial pace until reaching a tipping point whereupon a sizable portion of the population could suddenly afford a car. China had created the communist version of a middle class. It was a small percentage of their population, but in China that could still mean a hundred million people.

All it took was a few early adopters, and that led to "Keeping up with the Joneses". Soon everyone in China's middle class was buying a vehicle to display their status. It's fascinating to observe which behaviors transcend all cultural boundaries.

Think back to when you were a teenager and first got a driver's license. Did you care whether gas cost 50 cents per gallon or a dollar? Probably, but you were out cruising regardless. The global economy was in a situation where hundreds of millions of people simultaneously received a driver's license for the first time. It takes quite a while for the supply chain to digest an event like that.

The Chinese Communist Party fostered this buying frenzy as it sought to become a major player in automobile manufacturing. It needed a domestic market for its vehicles, so it put its thumb on the scale by subsidizing the price of gasoline for its citizens. This sudden influx of millions of new drivers combined with artificially cheap fuel is the reason high prices had not yet cured high prices in the global oil market.

By the middle of 2008 though, oil producers had adjusted their output to compensate for the increased number of drivers, and now there were rumblings that the Chinese subsidies would soon be eliminated. The situation was changing. The writing was on the wall, but traders were slow to respond because they were shell shocked by the previous five years. Fear and greed.

It is not as simple as just recognizing that a commodity price has become overblown and is due for a correction, because that scenario may last weeks, months, or years. Investors must look for cracks in the foundation, signs that the other market participants are noticing the irrationality of the status quo, before easing into the trade. Changes occur very slowly, and then all at once.

I conveyed my position to Neil Cavuto and proclaimed that oil had finally topped out. I never plan my message for these appearances. I give my honest opinion on whatever subject comes up. This was just another interview that I would have quickly forgotten about if not for a certain person that was watching.

CHAPTER 25

GOLDEN STATE

Within a few weeks of my appearance on Cavuto, the price of oil backed off and went into a bear market. I then received an unsolicited phone call from the chief investment officer of a prominent Silicon Valley company. "JJ" as we called him, had seen the interview and wanted to discuss giving me some money to "play around with." In his parlance, this meant several million dollars, which would make him our largest client.

All our clients were wealthy, but JJ was in another league. During that first conversation he casually asked if I knew Peter Thiel. "Of course," I said, meaning that I had read plenty about the highly respected investor and cofounder of PayPal.

He interpreted my answer to mean that I knew Peter personally. "Oh great!" he replied, "Maybe we'll all get together next time you're on the West Coast." Apparently, they were close friends.

"That would be fantastic," I said sheepishly, "But I must admit that I meant I am aware of who he is, not that we are personally acquainted." It was a slightly embarrassing confession, but we had a laugh about it which broke the ice. Soon, I forgot that I was speaking with a billionaire, and we had a relaxed conversation.

JJ was ready to open his account immediately, but I suggested we meet face to face before funding it. I think this confused him because any other broker would have been eager to get their hands on his money right away. I already had a West Coast trip planned for the following month to meet with another client, so it would be easy to add a stop in Silicon Valley. We scheduled the meeting for the tail end of my trip.

I touched down in Los Angeles a few weeks later and was picked up by the limousine of a long-time client, Charles, at his insistence. It had been a good year, and he was eager to show his appreciation. Charles rolled out the red carpet, taking me to the famous hot spots around the city. We had a lunch reservation at a place where he guaranteed we would encounter celebrities. I wasn't particularly interested in celebrities but was happy to play along. It seemed important to him, and I guess it would've been interesting to see Julia Roberts or the like.

Charles pointed out at least a dozen television actors and pop singers, none of whom I was familiar with. He was oddly embarrassed by the lack of A-list stars. I tried to play down the situation until a random passer-by, who happened to work in the commodity futures industry, recognized me from television and stopped to say hello.

It turned out that I was the biggest celebrity there, which Charles and I both found hilarious. We talked business for a few hours, and it couldn't have been more pleasant. By the end of our visit, I was feeling as confident as I ever have, which was good because my next meeting was with JJ, the tech magnate.

I landed in San Francisco the following afternoon and arranged my own transportation to his corporate campus. I went through a myriad of security checkpoints before meeting his assistant, who asked me to have a seat in the waiting room. I wasn't accustomed to waiting around like that, but since he was running a multi-billion-dollar enterprise I was willing to swallow my pride.

After a few minutes, his assistant informed me that we would have to cancel the meeting. Since I had come a long way, I asked if we could meet for literally one minute just to shake hands and look each other in the eye. It may seem like a pointless gesture to some, but you can learn a lot about a person during even a brief encounter. I wanted to give JJ the opportunity to size me up.

His assistant admitted he wasn't even in the building, which stung my pride. Again, I gave him some latitude due to the size of the company he was responsible for. Business crises can arise last minute, and he probably couldn't get away, or so I told myself. His assistant burst that bubble when she informed me that he had left early to attend his son's high school football game. That was a punch in the gut.

On some level I appreciated that a titan of industry was putting family ahead of business, but this meeting had been on the schedule for weeks. He could have cancelled before I arrived or tried to reschedule. The fact that he did neither led me to believe he was not seriously interested in becoming a client. The euphoria of self-satisfaction that I had experienced in Los Angeles had been diminished.

On my way back to the airport, I called Michael to give him the disappointing news: "JJ stood me up for our meeting, I guess we'll have to find another billionaire."

"That's interesting, because the bank wire just came through to fund his account," Michael replied.

It turned out that JJ appreciated my gesture of coming out there. He later apologized and said that attending his son's football game was important to him. They hadn't expected the team to make the playoffs, and the game was scheduled last minute. The fact that I showed up was all the due diligence he needed on me. With that, we had our first billionaire.

This West Coast trip reinforced some basic values: don't get too full of yourself when times are good, don't get too down on yourself when something doesn't go your way, and don't presume that you know what other people are thinking. Just do quality work, be professional, and let the chips fall where they may.

CHAPTER 26

PIQUE COTTON

The first edition of *The Complete Guide to Option Selling* had been a surprise hit, so our publisher stepped up the promotional efforts for the second edition in 2009. In the months leading up to its release, we scheduled several whirlwind trips to New York, where I was interviewed by seemingly every financial media outlet.

During an appearance on Fox Business, Liz Claman made me blush when she congratulated me on having called the top in the oil market by saying, "This is the guy... he said, '$145 and we'll pull back down.' It happened. Can you tell me what we're going to find on Mars next?" The reference was to scientists having discovered water on Mars, which was a topical story that day.

During those trips I also spent time with some of the biggest money managers in the world, which is something I didn't get to do very often in Tampa. There was value in that, so I started travelling to New York and Chicago more frequently.

Among the industry leaders with whom I met in Chicago were the proprietors of various Futures Clearing Merchants. FCMs are the large financial institutions that provided trade-clearing services for our clients and acted as custodian of their funds. A great advantage of the CTA business model is that we outsource these back-office operations, leaving us streamlined to focus solely on market analysis and trading.

I was always on the lookout for the best provider of FCM services for my clients. One of the people I met in this pursuit was Russell Wasendorf, the owner of an Iowa-based FCM called Peregrine Financial Group. I viewed it as a positive sign that the firm located their home office in rural farm country rather than in the city, as most of its transactions were in Ag markets.

PFG was a well-known clearinghouse that had been around for 20+ years, and it was growing rapidly in market share. Wasendorf was known to roll out the red carpet for prospective clients, flying them on his private jet from Chicago to his Cedar Falls headquarters, which was an impressive glass office building that looked out of place as it rose from the endless cornfields. Trying to impress decision-makers to win their business was not unusual in the industry, but he seemed to be trying much harder than everyone else. Perhaps I should have been more curious as to why. PFG's fees were low, but it seemed like its strategy was to make up for that in volume. I authorized my clients to use Peregrine as their FCM.

Cotton prices had bottomed out following the financial crisis of 2008, and by 2010 were rebounding due to strong global demand. When investors think about demand from emerging markets, they tend to focus on staple food crops and energy. That is Phase One, but once citizens of the developing nation accumulate some wealth, they begin to grow a taste for luxury items that were previously unattainable, like spare clothing.

In the developed world, we take apparel for granted. We have closets and dressers full of clothing for various occasions along with washing machines to clean them in. When a garment gets torn, stained, or falls out of fashion, we donate or dispose of it. In Third World countries, clothing is not a disposable resource. People use the same garments for a lifetime, spending countless hours mending them. The ability to easily replace old clothing has created a remarkable improvement in quality of life for billions of people in recent decades.

This cultural shift caused demand for cotton to continue growing, even as it increasingly ceded market-share to synthetic fabrics. China and India are the largest producers of cotton in the world, but they're also the largest consumers. India's government limits exports to make sure it has enough for its domestic market. China is a net importer of cotton, and it maintains massive surplus stockpiles just as it does with other commodities. As a result, the global cotton market is very tight and can be influenced by a wide variety of factors. When a commodity is relatively cheap, but the supply chain is very tight, it is at high risk for a price squeeze.

The United States has long been a major producer of cotton. Nearly all of the domestic crop is exported, only to be reimported in the form of textiles. This is because the processing of cotton into fibers, and then fabrics, and then apparel is extremely labor intensive. It's cheaper to ship it overseas to be processed by cheap labor.

One cannot discuss cotton without mentioning its impact on the deplorable history of slavery. The invention of the cotton gin in 1793 made processing the fibers more cost effective, but human hands were still needed to pick it in the fields. This probably extended the otherwise dying practice of slavery in the United States by decades. The embargo of Southern cotton is what ultimately bankrupted the Confederacy and ended the Civil War.

The sad truth is that slavery is still rampant in the cotton industry in many parts of the world, with up to 20% of the global supply being either picked or processed by forced labor. Raw cotton that is delivered in accordance with The New York Mercantile Exchange futures contract is required to have originated in the United States, which helps ensure ethical labor practices.

If you were only looking at the supply side of the equation for cotton, you'd see that 2011 was poised to be a record global crop, 40% larger than the previous year. That sounds like a bearish indicator. Demand was growing too, but not by 40%. There was expected to be more than enough product to meet global demand. But despite all this, the price of cotton rallied toward the end of 2010. Growers took that opportunity to sell their crop well in advance, locking in what looked like a nice profit.

Streamlined manufacturing and just-in-time inventory means that manufacturers need the commodity precisely when they need it. A few months sooner or later and the whole mechanism falls apart. Cotton prices can be impacted by a variety of seemingly unrelated weather patterns in different parts of the globe. If there are monsoons in India, or colder-than-expected temperatures in China, or a drought in Texas, supplies suffer. The market can absorb some of this, but not all at once.

When it appeared this perfect storm trifecta might occur, cotton prices began to soar. Futures peaked at $2.27 per pound in March 2011, the highest level in more than a century. Textile manufacturers had to either pay a hefty premium to secure the cotton they needed or scale back their production plans.

The actual cotton harvest in 2011 ended up being 15% larger than 2010, but the excess supply hit the market too late. With textile production already scaled back, and indeed some manufacturers had gone out of business, there was nobody to buy the product which had been in such high demand only weeks earlier. The price of cotton ended the year at less than one dollar. It was another lesson in the importance of timing when trading commodities. Investors often have a generally solid analysis of a commodity but get the timing wrong by just a few weeks, which can make all the difference.

I spent more time following the cotton market that year than probably any other commodity but could not bring myself to sell call options during the height of that rally. While that would have turned out to be a very lucrative trade, I simply did not have enough clarity of the situation until after the fact. Hindsight cannot be the determinant of whether the right decision was made. That assessment must be based on the information that was available at the time.

There is inherent risk in selling options, so I was extremely discerning in selecting which opportunities to take advantage of. That meant missing out on the high risk/high reward situations, which was okay. Our strategy involved base hits, not swinging for the fences. Unfortunately, even the most conservative trading strategy could not have protected us from the next big storm that was gathering in the distance.

CHAPTER 27

SWEET HOME CHICAGO

C ommodity futures are the purest of exchange-traded securities. Participants in this market speculate on the future
value of tangible products, so they typically don't worry
about unscrupulous CEOs cooking the books - which happens
frequently in equity markets. A bushel of wheat futures is stan-
dardized and not designated to come from a specific farm. The
buyer is not putting their faith in an individual to deliver on a
promise, but rather in the entire agricultural system. The system
is decentralized by nature, but it falls short of being perfectly
efficient or completely invulnerable to corruption.

In 2011, futures commission merchant, MF Global, was found
to have diverted client funds to cover margin calls in its own
trading account. The company went bankrupt, and customers
were left holding the bag. For several years leading up to that,
there had been rumors swirling about suspicious practices at the

firm. I viewed its collapse as vindication of my decision not to do business with them. Instead, most of my clients had accounts with PFG, which had an excellent reputation.

Liberty Trading was a success beyond anything I could ever have imagined, and I was determined to remain true to the values and principles that had gotten it to that point. I had seen too many hedge fund managers grow too fast too quickly, surround themselves with yes-men, insulate themselves from opposing viewpoints, and start to believe they were infallible. I would remain vigilant, scrutinize my strategy, listen to diverse opinions, and keep my ear to the ground.

With that in mind, I rented a condo in the newly built Trump International Hotel and Tower on Wabash Avenue, within walking distance of CME headquarters and The Chicago Board of Trade. The city had changed a great deal in the decade that had passed since I last lived in the region. The exchanges, which had previously been populated largely by individuals risking their own capital, were now staffed entirely by employees of multi-billion-dollar conglomerates and hedge funds. Instead of decision-makers, they were cogs in a machine relying on their handheld computer tablets to tell them what to trade. I quickly realized I wouldn't find much useful information on the trading floor.

While its proximity to the commodity exchanges turned out to be of little value, the condo in Trump Tower was useful in and of itself. The building was new and noteworthy, and people wanted to check it out. Rolls Royces lined the valet area, celebrities stayed in the hotel, and titans of industry dined at the Michelin-starred restaurant on the 16th floor with sweeping views of downtown and Lake Michigan. On more than one occasion, after stepping off the elevator, an associate mentioned that a "star" player from the Chicago Bulls had been riding with us. Several professional athletes lived in the building, but I never recognized anyone from those 2011 Chicago teams.

I had spent a lot of time in Chicago back in the 1980s and 1990s, and I can't imagine anyone ever shared an elevator with Michael Jordan without knowing exactly who he was. I suppose that's the difference between a star and a superstar.

I was once at a restaurant where MJ was dining in a private room. Every head in the place was turned in that direction as they ate, hoping to catch a glimpse of him. On another occasion, I was at a White Sox game when word circulated through the crowd that Jordan was in the press box. Soon, everyone was wrenching their necks upward to see if it was true rather than watching the game. He was larger than life, and still is, decades after his last retirement.

Billionaires are akin to superstar athletes. Michael Jordan, Tom Brady, Warren Buffet, Elon Musk. There is an indefinable quality to them, a presence. You can't help but keep your eye on them, to study them, to try to understand how they achieved super-stardom. I wanted to know what the billionaires were doing and why. With our client in Silicon Valley, we had a sliver of access to that elite club of investors.

It was no longer beneficial to speak with floor traders and eight-figure portfolio managers about their take on the markets. Those were the journeymen and utility players, deserving of much respect but not capable of carrying an organization to a championship. To play like a champion, I would have to train like a champion. I made a conscious effort to focus on the work that had gotten me into the big leagues in the first place, which was exhaustive research and independent analysis. When I wasn't training to be an MVP, I would be in the luxury box with the owners and general managers. That is where new ideas were discussed and strategies were implemented.

CHAPTER 28

THE OPTION SELLER

From our newsletter and our video series, which Michael Gross had been spearheading, we learned that delivering our message directly to the audience kept them more engaged. Without the filter or time constraints of legacy media, it was possible to have more substantive discussions. I spoke at a few book signings and small investor gatherings. The feedback was positive, so I agreed to speak at the nation's premier investment convention, The MoneyShow, in Las Vegas.

At The MoneyShow, I addressed a few hundred people. It was the largest live crowd that I performed in front of since being booed off stage with The Chainsaws in 1981. During my presentation there were no applause breaks, laughs, or even a cleared throat. Aside from my amplified voice, there was complete silence in the room. I feared I had lost the audience, that I was boring them, but it turned out they were listening intently. When I finished, there was an ovation followed by a lively Q&A session. It seemed everyone in that audience had already read my book, and they asked thoughtful follow-up questions.

That encouraged me to speak at another conference in Palm Beach that focused on the commodity futures industry. They set up a booth for me to autograph copies of my book and meet some of my readers – just as they did for many other authors.

During the event, I was approached by a legend in the commodity trading industry. Jim Rogers co-founded the Quantum Fund with George Soros in 1973 and wrote the seminal book, *Hot Commodities*, which is required reading for anyone new to this business.

Wearing his signature bowtie, Rogers asked, "So, you're the Option Seller?" Then he pointed at my book, which was on display behind me, and quipped, "I guess the secret is out."

He was lightheartedly referring to an open secret in the investment industry, which is that billionaires and institutional investors grow their net worth by selling options. They don't necessarily sell exchange-listed securities like I do. They might sell OTC (over the counter) options, swaps, insurance policies, and other complex means of collecting risk premiums. Most of the literature for retail traders, on the other hand, tended to focus on *buying* options.

Warren Buffet is known as a great stock picker, and he frequently extolls the virtues of compound interest. But it is no coincidence that all his investments fall under the umbrella of an insurance company, Berkshire Hathaway. Insurance premiums generate the cash-flow to make investments in other areas. That's how the rich get richer.

I shrugged and said, "Just kicking ass and taking names, Jim." a quote from the movie *Wall Street* that I'm not sure he picked up on. I was trying to play it cool, even though I was speaking to an icon.

Rogers patted me on the shoulder and said, "I bet you are! Keep it up," as I eagerly handed him a signed copy of *The Complete Guide to Option Selling*.

Russell Wasendorf from Peregrine Financial Group was also in attendance. I had last seen him on his private jet when we flew from Iowa back to Chicago, but I dealt with his son regularly. Most of my clients had migrated their accounts over to PFG by then, making me one of its largest Introducing Brokers.

Russell was overly nice to me, as usual. He had been working the room, gladhanding everyone he encountered. I knew Wasendorf pretty well, or at least I thought I did. He constantly tried to impress people by name-dropping the high-profile investors he did business with. He offered to introduce me to, of all people, Barbara Bush.

Not bad for a kid from Sturgeon Bay

Wasendorf had some connection to the former First Lady, and his limousine was waiting to bring him to an event at the Bush compound in Boca Grande. He invited me along, but I would have had to cut my meet-and-greet a few minutes short and leave right away.

I still had about a dozen people waiting to have their books signed, and I knew that each of them would want to speak with me for a couple of minutes. So, I politely declined the invitation.

It was probably for the best. I was not interested in being seen as political. I tried never to discuss politics or religion — at least not in public. That was not my job. I had clients and friends on both sides of the aisle. When Michael Jordan was criticized early in his career for refusing to endorse a Democrat politician, his response was, "Republicans buy sneakers, too."

There were other reasons to be cautious about making political statements. All registered investment firms must comply with a myriad of regulations and submit to occasional audits by regulatory agencies. Once every few years, the NFA would send over a team of accountants who set up shop in our spare office for a week while they reviewed our trade records and other documents. It was an understandable requirement for them to conduct their oversight, just another aspect of doing business, but beginning in 2009 the audits began to occur more frequently.

Strangely, I noticed that it was no longer the NFA or CFTC showing up at our door, but agents from a federal agency. We couldn't figure out why this was happening, but we always cooperated with them. We didn't know what the government was looking for. They always left after a few days without having found it. They always assured us we had been selected randomly and that it was standard procedure, but they kept coming back.

We were a boutique firm that didn't have an in-house accounting or legal department, so accommodating the investigators was a major distraction for my busy staff. I politely asked one of the agents if there was anything we could be doing differently that would stop these "random" investigations from being triggered. I thought perhaps we had filed paperwork incorrectly, received a complaint, or unknowingly failed to comply with a regulation. He told me — off the record — that the problem was our name: Liberty Trading.

When I chose the name in 1999 it had been a reference to my own liberty, having just become my own boss. After the terrorist attacks in 2001, a lot of companies began using patriotic-sounding names to capitalize on the public sentiment, which watered down the meaning of it. When the Tea Party Movement emerged, groups with patriotic names were viewed with suspicion by the Obama Administration. The agent told me flat out that if we changed our name, the audits would likely end. I found that hard to believe and dismissed it as nonsense.

We had created the website OptionSellers.com a few years earlier to promote the book and started using that domain as the website for Liberty Trading. During an interview on Bloomberg Television, journalist Pimm Fox asked why we didn't just name the firm OptionSellers. He was half kidding, but it was a great idea. Liberty had personal meaning, but it didn't say anything about what made us unique. It was important that potential clients understood what we did. OptionSellers was concise, accurate, and memorable. It left no doubt about the trading strategy we were pursuing.

In 2012 the National Futures Association (NFA) transitioned its auditing process to a more advanced system, likely in response to the MF Global fraud. As a result, we discovered why PFG had been so aggressive in recruiting clients. Russell Wasendorf had stolen $200 million from customer accounts, including my clients, and had been covering it up by photoshopping the account statements in his regulatory filings. He admitted everything in a suicide note, though his attempted suicide was unsuccessful. A shockwave reverberated through the commodity trading world. Everyone, it seemed, either had clients with money at PFG or dealt with a broker or trading partner that did. Liquidity dried up, and many brokerage firms were unable to recover.

Customer funds in commodity futures accounts should be seg-regated, meaning the custodian of the funds (Futures Clearing Merchant) cannot trade the money for its benefit. That is what made this such a punch in the gut. The market gave us enough risk to contend with, without the additional concern of our financial institution defrauding us.

PFG clients had their portfolios force-liquidated and were unable to trade or access their accounts for months, though they eventually had much of their stolen money returned to them after the government seized Wasendorf's assets. He was sentenced to 50 years in prison for his crime and will almost certainly never see the light of day. The NFA and CFTC have since implemented a system whereby they can electronically view account balances in real time to prevent this situation from happening again.

CHAPTER 29

BACK ON BOARD

The fraud committed by futures clearing merchants MF Global and Peregrine Financial Group rocked the commodity futures industry. Firms that had relied on those companies were abruptly forced to suspend their trading activities. Confidence in the system was shaken, investors shied away, liquidity suffered, regulations tightened, and commodities were about to enter a bear market. It was not a good time to be a commodity broker.

OptionSellers had always been something of a boutique firm, with just a few hundred clients. After PFG, we were a fraction of our former size. Even the billionaire from California, who had more than doubled his money in three years, closed his account in frustration.

Keeping in mind that adversity is an opportunity for growth, I tried to focus on the silver lining. We were fortunate just to have remained in business, as some of our competitors had been forced to close shop entirely. This created an opportune moment to raise capital.

Michael and I committed to rebuild the firm larger than before. He redoubled efforts on our marketing strategy, and I agreed to pound the pavement in search of ultra-high net worth investors.

In that pursuit, I accepted an invitation to a gathering aboard a yacht in Naples, Florida, where I would meet high-profile investors and hedge fund managers. In the past I usually declined such networking invitations, but with Michael doing such great work on our marketing and client engagement, the least I could do was put on a nice suit and mingle with smart successful people.

As I made my way through the marina, I heard classical music coming from the boat. Once on board, I realized the sound wasn't coming from electronic speakers, but from a Steinway grand piano on the main deck being expertly played by a beautiful woman in an evening gown. It was a surreal moment as I recalled my brother Patrick's comment years earlier at the shipyard in Sturgeon Bay, *"Who the hell needs a piano on a boat?"*

I was eager to meet the prominent investors and flattered to find that many of them were equally eager to meet me. I never grew accustomed to getting recognized from television appearances. It doesn't happen very often in everyday life, but at investment industry events like this it was common. Stock market and real-estate investors love pontificating on commodity prices. Many of them knew me as "The Option Seller", and that was the subject they were most interested in discussing. Option trading in general, and option selling in particular, had become a hot topic among wealth managers, many of whom already sold equity options.

I put my best effort forth but did not necessarily expect this event to result in any new business. A few days later, however, we got a call from one of the world's most accomplished portfolio managers. I must have met one of his representatives, though I was unaware of it at the time.

Billionaires who make their fortune in the investment industry are a different breed, and they are not as easily won over as the *nouveau riche* of Silicon Valley. Rather than having attained their wealth on one big idea, they built their fortunes methodically by making thousands of wise decisions over the course of decades. To achieve that kind of long-term consistency, they tend to be meticulous about their investments.

When dealing with such highly empowered individuals, I make no attempt to persuade them. People who have risen to that level have developed a strong ability to differentiate signal from noise, and they don't listen to sales pitches. The best way to connect with them is to concisely explain the strategy, methodology, risk profile, and past performance. They will evaluate for themselves. Only facts can persuade them, everything else is just small talk, and they don't have time for that.

We met in the famed investor's office, and he proceeded to ask for my outlook on markets. Commodity prices were down overall on the year, and I explained why I expected them to continue falling for the foreseeable future. He listened politely, but never gave any indication as to what he thought of my analysis. I left his office with no clue as to whether I'd hear from him again.

A few months after that first meeting, I received another invitation to the billionaire's office. He noted that my forecast had turned out to be correct, congratulated me on having another good year, and opened an account with my firm. One of the most successful portfolio managers in the world was hiring me to manage a small portion of his investments. It is an honor every time a new client puts their faith in me, but even more so when it is someone so accomplished in the same field.

Several of our wealthiest investors made a habit of calling me during the first week of January each year to discuss our performance from the previous year. One client in particular liked to call on New Year's Day. After not hearing a word from them for 12 months, and wondering whether they were even paying attention, they would get me on the phone to either congratulate me on a successful year or question why we had underperformed expectations. It turned out they were paying very close attention to my trading decisions.

They asked about transactions or events from months earlier. Why did we short soybeans in May? Why did we go long on silver in August? What were my thoughts on a particular USDA crop report or FOMC meeting?

They just wanted to talk shop, make sure that I had logical motives for my trades, and try to haggle over commission rates. It reminded me of my high school football coach putting me on the hot seat, questioning my decisions from the previous game, before tossing me the ball and telling me to get back out there and keep up the good work.

I learned to enjoy these conversations, because it meant that they were paying attention to what I was doing. I presumed they were scrutinizing their entire team of investment advisors in the same way and comparing the results. I liked the way I stacked up. Over time they allocated more money to my firm and recommended us to their friends and colleagues.

CHAPTER 30

WIND IN OUR SAILS

O ne of our goals as a firm was to provide our clients with plenty of information about the motives behind our trade decisions. Some investors paid close attention to every piece of data that we published, while others cared only about the year-end profit statement. Most fell somewhere in between. By making our material available to the public at large, we attracted new investors who were interested in learning more about our firm. Occasional print articles, television appearances, radio, and podcasts also helped get the message out.

The greatest client engagement tool that we had was our book, *The Complete Guide to Option Selling*. In 2014, we released the third edition and set out on another round of promotion. Ever since its initial publication 10 years earlier, colleagues have asked why I chose to divulge my trading strategy to the public. To them it made more sense to keep everything close to the vest, to avoid being copied.

It was true that my method of selling options could be replicated, it was simple in theory, but the choosing of the commodity and time horizon is where I had an edge. By thoroughly understanding fundamental and technical factors, I was consistently able to forecast markets accurately and be among the first to identify an opportunity. If other traders followed me in a few days later, so be it. That is an annoyance all successful portfolio managers must contend with. The benefits of our open-book policy greatly outweighed any drawbacks that came with it, and we continued to find new ways to engage the public.

By frequently releasing three-minute video market updates for all to see, I kept clients informed more efficiently. If there was a shakeup in the market, they were able to see my reaction the same day. Though these were complex issues that could not be thoroughly dissected in three minutes, I was usually able to get to the heart of the matter.

I never rehearsed for the videos. My assistant would enter my office in the afternoon, after markets had settled, and set up a small camera on a tripod. I took a minute to gather my thoughts, and then rattled off whatever came to mind.

Delivering so much material helped cultivate a stronger relationship with clients because they could see, hear, and read my analysis of the markets on a regular basis. When we eventually did speak personally, all their basic questions and concerns had already been addressed. This led to more substantive conversations, and the building of relationships.

Clients were free to withdraw their money without penalty. I believed having that freedom was important for establishing trust. However, the portfolio strategy was designed to work best with a long-term investment. My strategy involved holding short option positions in multiple commodities with overlapping time horizons of up to 24 months, and roughly 50% of the account in cash reserves. Unexpected withdrawals necessitated a rebalancing of the portfolio, which can negatively impact the return on the investment.

As OptionSellers continued to grow, it made financial sense to focus on recruiting only extremely high net worth investors. They take a longer-term approach to their investments and possess the risk tolerance necessary for commodity option trading. Michael and I considered raising the minimum investment to $1 million to improve the efficiency of the firm. Ultimately, we felt that would be too exclusionary, so we settled at $250,000 and continued providing educational resources for do-it-yourself traders free of charge.

Michael oversaw the selection and onboarding of new clients, which was a lengthy process to determine suitability. It began with the prospective client reaching out to us to request information. Our back office would send them our marketing materials, including a series of educational packets, questionnaires, performance history, and risk disclosures. If they were still interested, they would schedule a consultation with Michael. We gave prospects the opportunity to evaluate us as we were evaluating them.

It was a slow-paced, no-pressure approach, which most people seemed to appreciate. Others wanted to invest immediately and found the process to be frustrating. We were attempting to establish client relationships that would last decades, so if it was a problem for them to wait a couple of weeks before getting started, we viewed that as a sign it might not be a good fit. That was a mistake, and it caused us to lose a fair number of clients over the years. When Rosemary came on board, she put an end to that.

Rosemary Veasey was the office manager for OptionSellers and is still one of my top associates. She is the most delightful person you could ever meet. Clients loved her charming disposition and self-deprecating humor, which helped quite a bit when assisting them over the telephone with tedious account forms, documentation, and wiring instructions. I have always believed in surrounding myself with the best people, and Rosemary is the best at what she does. With her running the office operations, prospective clients no longer slipped through the cracks.

The final step before we commenced trading a new account was for the client to have a meeting or phone call with me. The purpose of that conversation was to ensure that the client understood the risks and had realistic expectations. It was redundant because Michael always covered these topics meticulously during his consultations. I loved having the opportunity to meet every client personally and get to know a bit about them and their business.

The three things I heard most on these calls were: 1) "Yes, Michael already mentioned that" 2) "*The Complete Guide to Option Selling* is the best investment book I have ever read" and 3) "Whatever you're paying Rosemary, you need to double it!"

I learned to predict what type of client someone would be based on these discussions. I got an indication of whether they would be around for the long haul, or if they would jump ship after experiencing the first drawdown. Some clients were going to call every day with a concern, or withdraw funds too frequently, or piggyback my trades in their online brokerage account. When you're new in this business, you'll take any client you can get. I was in position to be selective about who I did business with, and as a result we had the greatest clients in the world.

The most experienced investors often had one additional question, which always struck me as odd. They asked if I had suffered a major crash during my career as a portfolio manager. I had my share of losing trades, and even a few down years, but nothing that would be considered a crash. I didn't realize it at the time, but this had not been the answer they were hoping to hear.

CHAPTER 31

TIED KNOT

I had my share of serious girlfriends over the years, but never felt the clock was ticking for me to settle down. I had been a fun-loving thirtysomething, then fortysomething, then fiftysome-thing, never afraid that time was passing me by. I had a great circle of friends, lived in two amazing cities, Tampa and Chicago, and became a large player in the industry I had cherished all my life.

Of course, I was interested in finding the love of my life... I just hadn't met her yet.

In December 2015, just before making my annual trek north to spend the holidays with my family, I was invited to a big corporate Christmas party thrown by a prominent Tampa realtor. I wasn't enthusiastic about the idea at first, as I was scheduled to fly to Chicago the very next day. But I thought, *don't be a scrooge, in a few days you'll be in Sturgeon Bay, wishing you had some fun parties to go to.* So, I went.

Shortly after arriving, I spotted two of my good friends, Jim and Gio. They're both in real estate, as were most people attending. We shook hands, wished each other a merry Christmas, bragged about how amazing the year had been, and ordered a glass of holiday cheer. It hadn't been more than 10 minutes when they both drifted away to palm press their colleagues and any potential home buyers in the crowd.

I was standing there all alone when I noticed a very attractive woman who looked like she had arrived straight from work. She was wearing secretary glasses, a conservative green dress, and ankle-high black leather boots. She was all by herself near where I was standing, and it was difficult to take my eyes off of her.

I thought to myself, *"Go find your friends, James. She probably receives unwanted attention all the time. Besides, she's too young for you."*

That discouraging thought was shattered when we made eye contact. She gave me a big warm smile, walked right up, extended her hand, and said, "Hi, I'm Krista."

"Very nice to meet you. I'm James."

She had also been invited by Gio, whom she knew from church. We chatted for a few minutes, and then went our separate ways.

The following day I started preparing for my trip. I checked the weather in Chicago. It was cold, nothing unusual for December. Then out of the blue I received a text from Jim, asking if I planned on coming by to watch the football game. He added, "I think Krista might show up as well." Interestingly, that made all the difference, and I changed my plans.

I showed up to find a group of 10 people, all couples. When Krista arrived, we were the only singles there. I learned that she grew up near Cleveland and was a huge football fan. In addition, she worked for a financial company, so we had plenty to talk about. The ice was broken and, three hours later, I asked for her number.

The next day I flew to Chicago and spent a couple days celebrating the upcoming holidays with old friends before my four-hour drive north to Sturgeon Bay to be with my family. All the while Kriss and I were chatting several times a day. We decided to make it a date when I returned to Tampa. Somehow, we decided on New Year's Eve for a first date. No pressure there!

Jim was throwing a party to ring in the new year. Both Kriss and I knew many of the people who would be attending, so I asked if she wanted to stop by.

We were enjoying a glass of champagne, and the evening was fast approaching midnight. Somehow, at this point we were still holding hands. While there were perhaps 100 people there, we were now in a somewhat secluded area with maybe a dozen close friends. Jim asked the room, "What is everyone's New Year's resolution?"

When it was my turn, I blurted: "I do believe I'll be getting married this year!!!"

The small crowd gasped. Kriss, laughing nervously, tried to calm everyone by saying, "Hey, don't look at me. It must be the champagne talking!"

After spending decades looking for the girl of my dreams, it took less than a week to realize that I had found her. I remember wishing that my mother, who had passed away about five years earlier, could have met her. She would have loved Kriss like one of her own.

My father certainly did, and they got along incredibly well. He was in his late 90s at the time but was still exceptionally sharp. I recall bringing her to meet him several times while we were still dating. Kriss would often play cards with him, which was his favorite hobby. On several occasions Kriss asked my dad to tell her stories of his sailing days on the Great Lakes.

My dad assumed she was just being polite. No one had asked him to recount those stories for many years. He didn't understand why she would care, but she genuinely did. I remember him basically ignoring her the first few times. After multiple requests, he started telling her some fascinating maritime stories — some of which even I had never heard before. He was slightly hard of hearing, so Kriss would sit on the floor next to his easy chair.

In October 2016, less than 10 months after we first met, we were married at St Joseph's Church in Sturgeon Bay — the same place where I had attended parochial school, just one block from my childhood home.

I wondered how my business life would blend with married life. Professionally, I had been living out my dreams on a daily basis for years. Would there be room for more? What would that even look like? Well, I had just taken the leap, and I was about to find out fast.

Practically every morning started the same way. I'd find a tri-folded copy of the WSJ next to a cup of coffee in the kitchen. I actually prefer the hard copy to the e-version because the most valuable articles are usually buried in the later pages. Kriss would be expertly preparing breakfast for two. (Who would have guessed quiche could be baked in the shape of a heart?) The only thing she needed from me to start my day was an answer to her question: "Would you like to watch Bloomberg, Fox or CNBC?" Kriss knew how important it was for me to be aware of any major market developments. My firm was producing Alpha for our clients, and from her business background she understood that was pretty rare.

On many occasions while I was reading the paper, I glanced over and Kriss would be reading my trading books. She'd catch me looking at her and ask, "Why are you smiling?" My favorite time was when she looked up from a textbook and asked, "James, what's the difference between backwardation and contango?" That made my smile grow even larger. *Boy, did I marry the right girl!*

CHAPTER 32

FULL THROTTLE

O n election night 2016, Krista and I went to a bar in Tampa that was having a watch party for the Hillsborough County Republicans. We expected to lose graciously, drown our sorrows just a bit, and then wake up the next day and get back to work. Life goes on, after all.

Hillsborough is a pivotal county in the ultimate swing state of Florida, so it garnered a small amount of national attention on election night. I was surprised when Adam Shapiro, a reporter from Fox Business Network walked in the door followed by a cameraman and recognized me. He was as surprised as I was.

As previously mentioned, I don't like to comment publicly on politics, but there was no avoiding it that night. About five minutes after Florida and Ohio had been called for Donald

Trump, stock market futures were tanking in the overnight session. Neil Cavuto sent it over to Adam to get my thoughts.

"We're watching the futures market," I said, "and for some reason people are selling stocks because it looks like Trump is going to win. I think that's not such a good idea." Then I held up my glass in celebration on live television.

Unbeknownst to me, Michael posted the clip to our website and YouTube page the next day. When I found out, I thought that half of our clients would be furious. I waited for the complaints, but they never came. As heated as political discourse can get, I think most of us find in our own lives that we can be perfectly civil with people who disagree with us. Most of us have loved ones who voted for the other candidate, and it's a non-issue.

The year 2017 started strong for my business. And married life was better than I could have imagined. As summer approached, we made plans to spend a week in Ohio with her family, a week in Chicago with friends and colleagues, and finally a week in Wisconsin with my family.

After that first week in Akron, we decided to drive to Chicago rather than fly. We packed a small cooler and started the six-hour drive west. After a few hours we passed a sign that read, "Welcome to Indiana!"

Shortly thereafter, Kriss said, almost to herself, "The corn doesn't look so bad," as she peered out the passenger window. I asked what she meant, and she said, "I heard you speaking with Michael the other day about how dry it's been in the eastern corn belt. These fields don't look so bad."

She wasn't wrong. Kriss never lived on a farm, nor had I, but I'd been studying grains and soybeans for decades. "Kriss," I said, "You have a good eye for corn and soybeans, but the first few rows closest to the main road always look the best. The runoff of rain from the highway delivers moisture to the edge of the field. In order to forecast the yield for any given crop you need to walk several rows in."

Kriss suggested we do just that. I asked whether she was serious, and she replied, "Boots on the ground" — a phrase she had heard Michael and I say several times. We got off at the next exit and parked next to one of the largest cornfields in the area. We got out of the car and navigated the roadside ditch.

But before we could step one foot into the field, a pickup truck appeared out of nowhere. A man jumped out and said in a stern voice, "I'm going to tell you the same thing I told the other fella. We're not interested in selling!"

I told the proud owner, "We're not here to buy your land. We just want to see if the corn is tasseling on time. We heard it's been a dry start to the summer and wanted to see the condition of the crop."

"Well, why didn't you say so? I'll show you around."

Far from being a distraction, married life was actually making me a better market analyst.

The objective of market analysis and forecasting is not only to identify the most likely outcome, but also to assess all possible outcomes and their respective probabilities, then evaluate risk-versus-reward accordingly. The list of possible outcomes is infinite, so we proceed with an understanding that there are unknown risks that could potentially blindside us.

Investments are susceptible to risk from black swans, those rare and impactful events that almost nobody predicted, often because some widely accepted understanding of markets turned out to be false. Investments are also susceptible to grey swans, which are similar except for the fact that in hindsight they seem like they probably should have been foreseen. A perfect example was the 2008 financial crisis, when the red flags pertaining to subprime lending were ignored by all but a handful of traders.

Based on the type of investment, one can sense from which direction a grey swan is most likely to emanate. In agricultural commodities, major upheaval is typically weather-related. When industrial metals prices suffer a meltdown, it is most often caused by an unexpected downturn in the global economy. Energy, as a commodity class, is prone to volatility caused by unnatural forces.

Fossil fuel markets are periodically disrupted by geopolitical tensions, government regulations, production quotas, environmental activism, and technological developments. When drastic changes in supply and demand can be caused by a single government, cartel, grassroots organization, or corporation, as opposed to macroeconomic forces, they become more difficult to predict. Such events don't necessarily require widespread approval from consumers or voters, so they can seemingly emerge out of the blue. No other major commodity is as blatantly manipulated as crude oil. OPEC was specifically created for this purpose.

The United States is the world's largest consumer of energy, and one of the largest producers of fossil fuels, so it wields tremendous influence over the price of energy. The President's impact on the stock market can sometimes be overstated, but his ability to directly influence commodity prices is much greater. As an investor, you must be acutely aware of the current administration's policies, and what the downstream effect of those policies might be.

President Trump was not shy about wielding executive power to achieve his agenda. Expanding domestic energy production and using tariffs to renegotiate trade deals would have a major impact on commodity markets.

I found it strange that so many market prognosticators struggled to understand President Trump, because he seemed incredibly predictable to me. Like all politicians, he was going to act in his own best interest. Looking past the insults, hyperbole, and self-aggrandizement, you could generally count on him to follow through on his promises and threats, or at least attempt to.

Domestic oil and gas production, tariffs, diplomacy, taxes, dollar strength, and deregulation were all areas where Trump did exactly what he said he would do, but the broader market somehow never saw it coming. So many people were blinded by the sensational headlines that they failed to see there was low-hanging fruit everywhere. Trump's energy policy and trade war with China were creating ample opportunities, and I was seeing the market as clearly as I ever have.

My goal was to attain 20% annual returns for my clients while providing diversification from stocks and bonds. However, if a string of good fortune resulted in portfolios reaching that goal by August, I was not going to sit on my hands for the remainder of the year. I would continue taking advantage of opportunities as they presented themselves, knowing that there would be times in the future when we would underperform. I seemed to get everything right in 2017, delivering an average return of 58% for our clients.

Forecasting the market to perfection is an impossible goal, so we made sure that clients and future clients understood that 2017's rate of return would likely be an outlier. Regardless, our phones were ringing off the hook with investors wanting to join our family. Many of them had been reading our materials for years, thinking about opening an account, and seeing that 58% was the catalyst for them to finally sign up. Michael had a three- to six-month waiting list for consultations. We raised the minimum investment to $500,000 to reduce the number of applicants.

It had the opposite effect.

CHAPTER 33

FRACKONOMICS

O ver the span of nearly four decades — from the Hunt Brothers silver squeeze in 1979 until 2018 — I generated profits by taking calculated risks on commodity prices. I had made it through a gauntlet of market volatility unscathed by remaining vigilant about my risk strategy... and being lucky. I strived to identify potential risks in advance and was highly successful at it.

I felt like a quarterback reading the opposing defense perfectly, anticipating where the soft spots in the coverage would develop, instinctively sidestepping the looming pass rush, and throwing the ball to hit the receiver in stride just as he gets open. It may appear effortless in the moment, but that precision and confidence is a result of extensive preparation and experience.

Not every trade is profitable, just as not every play will result in a touchdown or even positive yardage. Sometimes, I settled for a field goal, threw it away, or got sacked, but I had always managed to avoid the costly interception.

I viewed my portfolio with the understanding that one or two of those positions were going to lose money. The key was for them to lose a little money instead of a lot. I strived to identify the losers and root them out as early as possible. Every position had risk factors that were closely monitored. If any of these risks came to fruition, or increased in probability, I had an exit strategy. I was patient and deliberate when getting into an investment, but I had a hair trigger about getting out when the risk assessment changed.

There were many times when I closed out of a position shortly after initiating it, because new information arose. On a few occasions, I had extolled the virtues of a commodity in our newsletter, but my forecast had changed by the time it went to press. By changing my stance, I risked looking foolish — especially if hindsight later revealed that the initial position would have made a profit. It didn't matter, I made what I determined to be the best investment decision for the client in real time.

I was a "check-down" quarterback, meaning that I was conservative. Clients sometimes asked why half of their account balance was sitting in cash. It seemed to many of them that we could have doubled our profits if we had invested all available capital. The excess cash served as dry powder, which we were free to deploy as new trade opportunities arose. The cash reserves also provided a cushion of equity to protect our clients from being issued margin calls, because occasional drawdowns were expected.

Being extremely selective about our portfolio, and proactive about risk management, kept us from getting hamstrung by a lack of capital. Discipline gave us flexibility to go after the most attractive trades.

During the late 20th century and the first decade of the 21st, natural gas earned a reputation for volatility. The price would often increase during early autumn, as speculators anticipated home heating usage during the upcoming winter. The price trended lower as winter arrived, only to rally again in the spring in anticipation of a hot summer causing increased electricity usage in the form of air conditioning. Demand forecasts were inconsistent, and the supply chain was unreliable.

In the United States, supplies of natural gas were particularly vulnerable to hurricanes because the critical infrastructure sites were in and around the Gulf of Mexico. Investments in drilling and pipeline construction carried high risk because they were both time and capital intensive, and there was no telling what the market would look like by the time a project was completed. The price of natural gas was low relative to the cost of extracting it from the ground and getting it to market. With slim margins and a tight supply chain, it's no wonder the price was volatile.

Then came the era of fracking when the supply chain grew larger and more fragmented. This technology enabled drillers to extract natural gas from deep beneath solid rock, opening new regions for oil and gas production. Hydraulic fracturing had been around for decades, but technological advancements brought about its more widespread use starting in 2008. Over the ensuing decade, natural gas gradually became one of the most abundant, and least volatile, energy sources.

Looking at a map of North America, it's difficult to find a region that does not have at least some natural gas production. Farmers and ranchers around the country found a new revenue stream in recent years as massive reservoirs were discovered deep under their land. Wildcatters searching for crude oil began finding natural gas by accident, and lots of it.

The increase in supply was so great that vast oilfields in North Dakota could be seen from space, burning off excess gas because it was not worth the expense of transporting it to market, or even capping the well. That situation can exist when natural gas is worth $2 per MMBtu (million British Thermal Units) or less. The calculus changes as the price rises, and all that excess gas starts finding its way to market. When the price reaches a certain level, trillions of cubic feet of natural gas begin flooding in from all around the continent.

This price elasticity is, to varying degrees, true of all commodities. High prices cure high prices. The difference was that natural gas now had an efficient infrastructure that could respond almost in real time. A shortage of wheat may encourage farmers to plant more of the crop next season, but the supply chain cannot begin to recover until the following harvest. Mining operations are expensive and take many years to set up, so the response to higher demand for copper might take a decade. Thanks to fracking, and the investments in infrastructure that it led to, natural gas producers could respond within days.

The fact that natural gas is relatively eco-friendly protects it, to some degree, from major legal challenges. Environmentalists bemoan all fossil fuels, but, if they are sincere about their concerns over carbon emissions, they much prefer clean-burning natural gas over coal-fired power plants. As a result, there is no threat of a law being passed to ban natural gas usage. The political risk to natural gas lies in the issuance of permits for drilling and pipeline construction. During the height of the Trump administration in 2018, that risk had all but disappeared.

Domestic natural gas production was booming and continuing to expand under the Trump energy policies which would be in place for at least two more years. Supply was abundant and the marketplace was efficient, but call options still carried inflated risk premiums as a vestige of the pre-fracking era. Just as with coffee in the late 1990s, many speculators were relying on outdated concepts.

While the long-term prospects for natural gas from one administration to the next are highly variable, within the confines of the 2018-2019 winter season it was clear to me what to expect. It was highly unlikely that the market would experience a major supply disruption in the short term. We endeavored to capitalize on this stability by selling out of the money call and put options.

Natural gas experienced average daily fluctuations of less than 1%, and our portfolio was designed to absorb daily price moves of over 10% without an issue. I believed that a rally greater than that would require a change in the fundamental drivers, which we monitored closely. By selling far out of the money call options, we stood to make money unless a *major* shift took place in the market. By choosing options with six months until expiration, we limited the time horizon for such a fundamental change to occur. That was the type of opportunity I was hired to seize on behalf of my clients.

Of course, there was still risk involved. Despite improvements and fragmentation of infrastructure, many of the natural gas pipelines still went through the Henry Hub in Louisiana. They can endure a run-of-the-mill hurricane, but a Katrina-type event could disrupt the supply chain for an extended period, so this was something to keep an eye on. A significant cold front would increase demand, causing natural gas prices to rise by a few percentage points, and a prolonged polar vortex would create substantially higher prices, so again this is something I paid extremely close attention to. There are dozens of data points relevant to natural gas, and I tracked all of them.

A tropical storm forming in the Atlantic, or a blast of frigid air moving south from Canada were things I could see coming at least a few days in advance. If the risk profile changed, I believed that I would be able to get out of the trade with a manageable loss. Willingness to accept a small loss was a key part of my strategy and had been a foundation of my long-term success up to that point.

CHAPTER 34

NATURAL GAS EXPLOSION

Early in November 2018 the price of natural gas began to drift higher in a seemingly unremarkable manner. We reevaluated the position, as was common practice whenever an underlying commodity drifted more than a couple of percentage points from our entry price. The first step was to identify what was pushing the market against us, because the root cause of the problem is a primary factor in determining the appropriate solution.

If the price increase were caused by a short squeeze in the futures market, for instance, that might be handled differently than if it were due to a genuine surge in demand for the commodity.

In this case, the market appeared to be reacting to a cooler forecast for North America over the ensuing weeks. The temperature adjustment was slight, and the impact on demand for natural gas would not be enough to materially change my seasonal outlook.

The following week, the rally accelerated. There was no apparent cause of the sharp move, and that uncertainty fueled panic among market participants. The price of natural gas seemed to be acting irrationally, but one cannot argue with the ticker tape. In keeping with our risk parameters, I decided to buy back all our short natural gas calls. In an illiquid fast market, that was no easy task.

Natural gas is normally among the most liquid commodity option markets, but on that day the bids and offers were scarce. Since nobody knew what had caused natural gas to spike in the first place, nobody could be confident that it wouldn't continue rising at that rate. Few were willing or able to sell us the options we needed to buy.

Though I failed to understand it at the time, OptionSellers was no longer a small nimble trading firm, anonymously moving in and out of positions with ease. We had grown to where we now had a significant influence on the market, so our buying fueled the rally even further.

There is an old trading cliché that I had managed to success-fully adhere to up until that point, which says you should "buy when you can, not when you have to." In the past, my ability to forecast commodity markets accurately had allowed me to avert danger by getting out of the way of market events early. I bailed out of trades at the first sign of trouble and lived to play another day. This time, however, I was blindsided.

The price of natural gas jumped nearly 50% in 36 hours. It occurred without warning or reason, and the losses we suffered were catastrophic. Even that large of a move would not have been enough to sink us if not for the total mystery surrounding the event. Our short call options were still, for the most part, well out-of-the-money — meaning they had no intrinsic value to them. The potential value, or implied volatility, however, rose to an extreme level that was far beyond commensurate with the increase in the underlying commodity price.

After years without a single OptionSellers account being issued a margin call, all our clients received one on the same day. The decision was made to begin closing all positions in all commodities, effectively shutting down the firm.

I experienced widespread negative attention for the first time in my career, which was to be expected based on the outcome of events. In a span of less than one week, I went from being considered a titan of the commodity option industry, to being compared with the captain of the Titanic. I accepted the criticism of people like Nassim Nicholas Taleb, a highly regarded mathematician and option trader who coined the term "black swan" in the context of financial markets. Taleb had long been an outspoken critic of the practice of option selling, so his opinion was in keeping with his established philosophy.

The loudest voices, however, were pundits and bloggers who knew little about the situation, had never been successful traders themselves, and had no allegiance to the truth. They wanted to generate clicks for their websites by any means necessary, which meant sensationalizing the story. There were implications that we had misled our clients, or that we had gambled away Granny's pension. The truth is that we were extremely forthright with our clients, all of whom were wealthy and experienced investors who understood the risks. I was tempted to publicly respond to the defamatory claims, but ultimately decided that it would do no good. The fact was that we had crashed, and the nuance of the story was unimportant. Public opinion no longer mattered, the only people who deserved an explanation were our clients.

The problem was that I had no explanation to offer them — the natural gas market had experienced no production outage, no major increase in consumption, no significant change in the weather forecast, no electronic trading mishap like the one that caused the flash crash in 2010. Nothing. Such a large price move without an identifiable cause was difficult to reconcile.

I recorded a video message for our clients, the text of which I shared in the beginning of this book, to explain the situation as best I could. The video soon made its way to the internet and the mainstream media, which had a field day with it. Oh, how the mighty had fallen.

It doesn't matter that the price of natural gas soon fell back within my target range, and every option that we had sold short eventually went on to expire worthless as expected. The price of natural gas was inflated just long enough to force me out of the position. The market remained irrational longer than I was able to remain liquid.

CHAPTER 35

FACING THE MUSIC

For the first time in my career, I did not want to face my clients. They were all sophisticated investors who knew that this result was a possibility, but none of us anticipated it. I spoke with dozens of them over the following weeks to explain what happened as best I could, and to answer any questions they might have, but mostly to accept responsibility.

I expected to eat crow during these calls, and in several instances I did. Some clients were angry, all of them were disappointed, and I completely understood. In most cases, however, I was overwhelmed by the amount of compassion they showed. Men and women who had just lost significant sums of money on a trade that I made were largely concerned with how I was coping with the situation. They asked how my staff was doing. They wanted to know when I would be reopening the firm, which was one of several questions I couldn't answer.

If only Bank of America and the FBI had been so forthright. Over the following weeks, as I had emotional conversations with clients and tried to deconstruct what had occurred with natural gas, I still had no access to my savings and no indication of why the feds were investigating.

Krista and I survived by using a credit card and envelopes full of cash which my father had left behind. After multiple failed attempts to get our account reopened, Bank of America scheduled a time for us to come pick up a cashier's check for the entirety of the account balance. The only problem was, no other banks were willing to let me open an account. Krista stashed that check in the liner of Abigail's carrier bag, knowing that she was the one thing we would never accidentally misplace. We thought it would be in there for a few hours. It ended up being a few weeks.

We were in Ohio, visiting Krista's family, when my accountant called to say that he found a small bank in Tampa that would let us open an account. The next morning, we flew back down to Florida, opened the account and deposited my life savings, and flew back to Ohio that evening. One of Krista's relatives was ill, and we wanted to remain by their side.

The following day, the new bank called to tell us they had to close our account. No explanation was given. We would soon be flying to Tampa once again to pick up another cashier's check which would also be stashed under our beloved Abigail. There were several iterations of this, where the rug kept getting pulled out from under us.

Henry Becker and Marc Kasowitz's attempts to find answers kept leading to dead ends. We never found out why I was de-banked multiple times. In January, we finally found an institution – Bay First Bank – that was willing to accept our deposit.

I had always been proud of the way I earned my money, so I wasn't shy about enjoying the fruits of my labor. I also have the sensibilities of someone raised in a big family in a small town, so I don't spend extravagantly. I drive a nice car, but it's not a Rolls Royce. I live in a nice house, but it's not a mansion. I fly first class, not private. I'll gladly spend a hundred dollars on a bottle of wine, but not a thousand.

Our boat, *The Krista Renee*, was the biggest exception to that rule. I have three great passions in life: commodity trading, boating, and my wife. Buying *The KR*, I thought, was a way to use my first passion to pay for something that served the other two.

In the aftermath of losing my client's money on that trade, the last thing I wanted was to be seen sipping champagne on the aft deck of my 72-foot luxury yacht.

People kept showing up at the Tampa marina to inquire about it and me. Eventually, I moved it to the marina in Naples where it would be less conspicuous among the mega-yachts – some of which were twice as big. What had been a crowning symbol of my success, turned out to be an albatross around my neck. We were never able to fully enjoy it. We took her out maybe a dozen times before deciding to sell.

As for the FBI, they never told us why they were investigating me. They refused to even confirm the fact that they were investigating. Eventually, those problems just went away. Henry was right again.

To have the greatest failure of my life compounded by false accusations, intimidation, and the threat of having my entire net worth unjustly confiscated, made it far more difficult to take responsibility for what I had gotten wrong. Fortunately, the intrinsic values instilled by my parents guided me through it. I couldn't run or hide from what happened.

Ray Dalio's book, *Principles*, helped me to realize that I wasn't alone. Dalio credits a similar crash which he suffered early in his career as being foundational to his later success. I finally understood why new clients sometimes asked whether I had ever suffered through something like that. They weren't looking for me to be infallible. They were looking for me to have perspective. They wanted someone who knew what that experience felt like, because that is the person they could count on to do whatever it takes to avoid being there again.

I know that most of my critics view me in the same light as the poker player who frequently goes all-in, risking everything to pick up just a few chips. They believe that I took big risks, and I was bound to run out of luck eventually. 'It works every time, until the last time,' they might say. From a distance, that is an understandable assessment of my situation. But I must push back a little.

I never went all-in. I didn't bluff. I folded quite often. But this isn't poker. Losses aren't limited to the chips you have in the center of the table. In this game, you can lose a hand so badly that even the chips stacked in front of you and the money in your pocket is lost too.

Allowing someone to manage any portion of your wealth is a tremendous act of trust. Money represents security and opportunity for your family, including future generations. I reminded myself of that often throughout my career and regarded the responsibility as sacred. That is why, although I was pained by the outcome, I was not ashamed of the way I conducted business. I was honest. I took the work seriously. I was vigilant. I always did what I believed was in the client's best interest. I adhered to the trading strategy... But I got blindsided.

CHAPTER 36

SET ADRIFT

E arly in my career, I believed that every outcome had a specific and identifiable cause, and a tangible lesson to be learned. I routinely combed through the details of my losing trades to see what I had gotten wrong, and how I could improve. As a result, I never made the same mistake twice.

When I decided to take a hiatus from running the trading firm, I anticipated being back in business within a year. I kept a small team on the payroll, anchored by Rosemary Veasey to run the office and Matthew Donovan to help formulate an improved trading and risk management strategy. I even held onto our office in the SunTrust Building, despite having no clients to entertain there.

I hold myself and my team to a high standard. We focus on long-term outcomes and try not to be unduly influenced by the sensational headlines or market reactions of a single day. The attributes which brought me success as a trader are that I have a Type A personality when it comes to research and analysis, but a great deal of patience when it comes to executing my strategy. I am cautious and skeptical, as one must be when selling options.

In keeping with that approach, I decided that OptionSellers would remain closed until I figured out exactly what we had gotten wrong, and why. I evaluated every major decision that we made leading up to November 2018. I took a closer look at the data that had been available at the time, searching for anything that could have been an indicator of what was about to transpire. Even with the benefit of hindsight we're still uncertain of the cause, however there is one hypothesis.

A forest fire that devastated California during the summer of 2018 was later found to have been the fault of Pacific Gas & Electric, a utility company whose power lines and transformers have been blamed for over 1,500 wildfires in recent years. Utility companies are large consumers of natural gas and, as bona fide hedgers of the commodity, they are likely to hold a large position in futures, options, or other derivatives as a hedge against their operating costs. The aim is to reduce their risk and provide stable returns for their shareholders.

The suspicious jump in natural gas prices occurred around the same time that PG&E management learned that they were at fault for the fire. They may have surmised that they would be facing billions of dollars in liability leading to bankruptcy, as later proved to be the case. This is mere speculation, but it's plausible that the company unwound a substantial position in natural gas derivatives that day, setting off a chain reaction of volatility that ultimately led to the parabolic move that did me in.

Forest fires are part of the natural cycle of the ecosystem and have been for millennia. Fires are one of Mother Nature's tools to clear out the dead in order to make room for new life. In modern times, the timber industry took over that role by clearing out old dry wood and making room for younger greener trees which are far less flammable.

Recall the spotted owl controversy from the 1990s, mentioned earlier in this book. Protection of the owl, and several other endangered species, has led to many old-growth forests remaining uncleared for decades. An unintended consequence of that action is that we are left with millions of acres of dry tinder, ready to go up at the drop of a match. Experts directly attribute the increased severity of fires in recent years to those wildlife protections.

That is not to say that I oppose conservation efforts. But natural ecosystems, like investment strategies, require balance. There is a complex butterfly effect wherein seemingly isolated events in one commodity have tremendous downstream impact on other commodities. The more I understand about it, the more I realize how much is left to learn. It is endlessly fascinating.

I was eager to reopen the firm but decided to wait until after the looming 2020 presidential election. Just because the ship has been built to withstand a storm does not mean that it would be wise to set sail directly into another hurricane.

It was clear that this would be no ordinary election cycle because the Trump administration had been such a significant threat to the entrenched global power structure. The Chinese Communist Party had been on a decades-long march toward geopolitical dominance and, prior to 2016, nobody seemed willing or able to stop them. China, Big Tech, the intelligence community, the military industrial complex, politicians, and oligarchs of all sorts were threatened by various Trump policies.

Those are immensely powerful entities, and all their interests were aligned. It seemed inevitable that something completely unpredictable was going to throw society into chaos before the election. I didn't know exactly what to expect, but when coronavirus emerged I thought to myself, "Oh sugar, this is it."

Never in my career had every market simultaneously experienced so much uncertainty. Even U.S. Treasury Bond markets suffered liquidity issues. Large swaths of the economy were shut down, and naive bureaucrats believed they would be able to restart them with the flip of a switch. The presidential election came and went, but the market impact of coronavirus remained. The global supply chain was in disarray.

The new administration's agenda was expected to increase regulations on many businesses, reduce domestic fossil fuel production, and raise taxes while much of the economy was still impaired by pandemic restrictions. The return of inflation was all but guaranteed, and stagflation began to look like a distinct possibility.

With the global economy on a precipice, it looked like a good time to hunker down and just park your capital in precious metals. I spent the next two years continuing to refine and test our commodity option selling strategy. As markets continued their strange behavior, I witnessed other notable traders experience crashes of their own.

Melvin Capital was a multibillion-dollar hedge fund run by Gabriel Plotkin, one of the smartest minds on Wall Street. Plotkin's pedigree included learning under two of the most successful hedge fund managers in the world, Ken Griffin and Steve Cohen, before starting his own firm in 2014. Melvin had excellent returns in its first several years, specializing in shorting the stock of retail companies it believed to be overvalued. Two of their biggest positions being in AMC movie theaters and GameStop.

Tired of being preyed upon in what they viewed as a rigged market, a large group of small investors — known as the Wall-StreetBets community on Reddit — got revenge by creating a short squeeze in the stock of AMC and GameStop. Melvin had exploited a quirk in equity markets which allowed them to short more shares than were available on the exchange, making it nearly impossible to close out of their positions during the parabolic rally.

The Reddit traders ran the stock of these relatively worthless companies up to absurd valuations. To my surprise, they were able to keep the stock prices inflated for an extended period, causing Melvin to suffer tremendous losses. Plotkin was probably correct in his analysis of GameStop as a retail company, they are still not selling very many video games, but he was overleveraged. It's not unusual for a short seller to get caught in a squeeze, but this was of epic proportions.

The rally temporarily subsided when Robinhood, a free online brokerage utilized by WallStreetBets traders, restricted investors from buying the stock on its platform. Discount brokerages are like social media platforms; they can be useful tools, but you must always remember that if you're not paying for the service, you are not their customer. You are their product.

The strange times continued as supply chain disruptions, lingering coronavirus restrictions, and a peculiar labor shortage impeded the economic recovery throughout 2021, yet stock and real estate continued to surge in value. Russia invaded Ukraine in 2022 and the price of crude oil, natural gas, corn, wheat, and gold reached multi-year highs.

In that environment, we came to expect an "unprecedented" event to occur every month or so. Rational investors have increasingly been turning to commodities as a hedge against runaway inflation and geopolitical instability.

Commodity markets have become more complex just as millions of new investors are flooding into them. Many traders know that there is money to be made in commodities and have a general sense of how to do so — but have yet to learn the idiosyncrasies and pitfalls of these markets. Even experienced commodity advisors and speculators are having a difficult time navigating this new landscape, as many of the old tried-and-true approaches no longer work. There is a greater need for Commodity Trading Advisors than ever before.

When OptionSellers ceased regular trading operations, we also stopped producing informational materials for the public. Rosemary dealt with an influx of phone calls and emails from do-it-yourself traders who had been following my analysis for years. They had come to rely on us.

The newsletters, tutorials, and market update videos had always been intended to keep our clients informed. Because the minimum investment to open an account with my firm was half a million dollars, it was not an option for most people. Tens of thousands of additional people from all walks of life, most of whom were not eligible to become clients, regularly found value in our materials. That was an unexpected outcome, and it was quite fulfilling.

There were young professional traders, college students, farmers, businessmen, retirees, and every other type of person you can imagine using our analysis to help inform their investment decisions. As a young man, I utilized a variety of free resources to educate myself about commodity markets, and it felt wonderful to pay that forward. Perhaps there was a future commodity titan out there learning from my experience. They didn't care about one bad trade; they cared about decades of honest analysis. They knew me and knew that I didn't dance for the media. There was still an audience for that.

Early in my career, market data was hard to come by. Nowadays, the problem is too much information. Investors are unsure of what they should pay attention to. Regardless of individual strategy or risk tolerance, many investors need help interpreting the signals and ignoring the noise.

To that end, as I waited for the right moment to reopen my trading firm, I resumed production of *The Cordier Commodity Report* as a website dispensing independent analysis and market updates which I believe to be useful to retail investors and professional traders alike.

CHAPTER 37

REFLECTION

Markets have always been subject to cycles. Not only the seasonal and economic cycles of which every trader is aware, but also cycles between complacency and hysteria. Complacency occurs in a stagnant or seemingly predictable market when investors feel safe but do not anticipate exceptional returns. Hysteria occurs during the panic of bear markets and the euphoria of bull markets, when investors let fear and greed override logic. The key to beating the market is to remain vigilant during times of complacency and opportunistic during times of hysteria.

We have all heard platitudes like, "the calm before the storm," or "it's darkest before the dawn," uttered with the benefit of hindsight. They're true, but the difficulty lies in recognizing these circumstances for what they are in real time. Stock market analysts always have "buy" ratings on market bubbles when they pop and "sell" ratings on bear markets long after they've bottomed out.

It is in our nature to vacillate between extreme caution and irrational exuberance. Human beings tend to overcompensate due to recency bias, loss aversion, fear of missing out, and groupthink. This is what causes the pendulum of public opinion to swing too far in the opposite direction after a disruptive event.

The goal of my research and analysis was always to stay ahead of these cycles, waiting patiently for volatility to reach its crescendo, and then riding the wave all the way down.

When I set out to open my own firm in 1999, there were plenty of doubters. My decision wasn't solely about making more money, it was about the pursuit of an idea. It was driven by intellectual curiosity as much as anything else. I have always been captivated by the fundamental factors, technical indicators, psychology, and rationale that drive commodity markets.

Over 30 years, I developed an understanding of which data points would have a meaningful impact on commodity prices and which ones wouldn't. I honed an ability to forecast long-term trends, as well as short-term market reactions, more accurately than my peers. I sought to find the most effective way to capitalize on that ability. That search led me to option-selling.

Sharing the billionaire's trading strategy with millionaires would put a target on my back from those wishing to keep it a secret.

Colleagues said that selling options — particularly naked options — was too risky. They believed I would crash and burn within a year or two, at the first sign of market volatility, just as others before me had.

Somehow, 19 years later, I was still going strong. This was despite holding short options at the onset of several market meltdowns; including the Y2K/tech bubble, September 11th, Mad Cow Disease, 2008 financial crisis and Great Recession, two FCMs defrauding investors and imploding, the most shocking election result in U.S. history, a multifront trade war which upended the global trade order, as well as countless droughts, heat waves, frosts, polar vortexes, and hurricanes.

How was it that, after all those years and all those black swans, a seemingly innocuous turn of events in natural gas ultimately took me down? That question haunted me for a long time.

The answer is, in a word, liquidity. I knew natural gas could experience extreme volatility. I knew that during such instances of extreme volatility, markets were going to become less liquid. I failed to realize the incredible extent to which they would become illiquid.

I had avoided being in that position for so long that I lost sight of how bad it can be. I was lulled into a false sense of security by the tremendous depth and reliability that natural gas option markets normally provided. Unconsciously, I started to believe that I would always be able to rely on that liquidity – or at least something reasonably close to it. That was my primary mistake.

In theory, the natural gas market should never have behaved the way it did during those three days in November 2018. In theory, there is no difference between theory and practice — but in practice, there is.

That is the reality I now face, but it is not as harsh as I feared it would be. I can't sit back and complain that the market did not do what it "should" have done. I can only accept what it did.

When we conducted the postmortem analysis in the immediate aftermath of the natural gas trade, I expected to find that we had made an operational error, like a key piece of data had been overlooked. That type of problem would have had a cut-and-dry resolution, and we would have been able to get right back to business. We found no such simple error, which meant there would be no quick fix.

Matthew and I reluctantly arrived at the conclusion that, regardless of how many data points had been analyzed, it would have been impossible to foresee the sequence of events that unfolded in the natural gas market that week. It was hubris to believe that I could have. After decades of remaining two steps ahead of the market, it had begun to seem like every conceivable risk factor was being monitored on my radar. The crash was a harsh reminder that I must be prepared for inconceivable risks, too.

It is not enough just to recognize that a particular market is mispriced. In order to drive the price back to fair value, we need other market participants to recognize it as well. Otherwise, it can remain irrational in perpetuity. So, we must wait for signs that cognitive dissonance has begun to dissipate before taking a position. That is what I have been waiting for, and I am in no rush.

Friends, colleagues, and clients have repeatedly asked when I plan to reopen my trading firm. As society has endured a series of destabilizing events over the last few years, my answer has been, "When the time is right."

My father continued doing the things he enjoyed — fishing, playing poker, smoking cigarettes, and watching baseball — right up until he passed away at the age of 99. He was an inspiration until the end. My passion is trading commodities, and I plan to do it until the day that I die. If Dad's longevity is any indication of my own, that would mean I have nearly 40 years left in this business. (Maybe more, since I've never been a smoker.) It is likely that I will encounter another black swan before my career is over, and I will be prepared. My crash in 2018 was the most powerful lesson ever given to me. As I embark on the next stage of my trading career, I do so with a deep knowledge, humility, and understanding of what it is like to be at the mercy of the market...

And I thought I was smart before.

TIME VALUE

When cracks in the global trade order became apparent in 2020, many investors opted for a flight to quality. Some went to gold and silver and, although they missed out on a melt-up in the stock market, they did just fine. Others chose the safety of bonds — and lived to regret that decision.

After my father passed away in late 2017, my siblings and I went to his house in Sturgeon Bay to clear out his belongings. In doing so, we uncovered some priceless black-and-white photographs and details about our family history. We also found many of his works of art, some finished and some unfinished. The biggest surprise was the envelopes of cash stashed throughout his house in sock drawers, toolboxes, and behind paintings. It wasn't a tremendous amount of money, just a few hundred dollars here and there. Dad was always prepared for rainy days. He was never a rich man, but he also was never late paying a bill in his entire life.

Ironically, Krista and I wound up using that cash to get by during those difficult weeks after we had been excommunicated from the banking system. My father's cautious, Great Depression-instilled values helped us survive. I will always remember that.

I also remember my great-grandfather Eugene Cordier's fate. By keeping his ship in port to wait out the storm, he ended up costing himself dearly. It turns out that if he had set sail earlier on that day in 1893, he likely would have avoided the storm altogether. His risk aversion cost him his ship, his cargo, and probably his livelihood.

Life, like trading, is about balance. There will never be a perfectly safe time to set out on a voyage. If I had avoided taking risks early in life, I would never be where I am today.

There was risk in selling my silver in 1980. There was risk in joining a band and moving to Madison. There was risk in packing up my car and driving to Chicago based on the handshake promise of a job. There was risk in creating my own approach to trading. There was risk in leaving a great job at Allendale to open my own firm. There was risk in getting married for the first and only time at the age of 54. There was risk in every trade I ever made. There is risk in every trade anyone ever makes.

An ability to manage risks, and choose the right ones to take, brought me everything that is good in my life. Opting to take the wrong risk on one occasion nearly cost me everything. I had lost my clients, my firm, my reputation, and millions of dollars. It didn't cost me my marriage – Krista has been by my side through all of it, and we've only grown stronger.

I kept my core staff in place for five years while my trading firm remained closed to investors. I never expected it to take that long. My team and I focused on research, analysis, and risk mitigation strategies to make sure this would never happen again. I waited years for the perfect time to relaunch. Eventually, I came to understand that there is no perfect time, but there is a right time – and it finally arrived.

In 2024, I reopened my office doors to invite a select group of clients to join Alternative Options — a new trading firm dedicated to true diversification by offering investors a viable alternative to the standard slate of stocks and bonds.